Pragmatics

Until 1995, George Yule was a Professor in the Linguistics Program at Louisiana State University. He now lives and writes in Hawaii.

Published in this series:

H. G. Widdowson: *Linguistics*
George Yule: *Pragmatics*

Oxford Introductions to Language Study

Series Editor H.G. Widdowson

Pragmatics

George Yule

OXFORD UNIVERSITY PRESS
1996

Oxford University Press
Walton Street, Oxford OX2 6DP

Oxford New York
Athens Auckland Bangkok Bombay
Calcutta Cape Town Dar es Salaam Delhi
Florence Hong Kong Istanbul Karachi
Kuala Lumpur Madras Madrid Melbourne
Mexico City Nairobi Paris Singapore
Taipei Tokyo Toronto

and associated companies in
Berlin Ibadan

OXFORD and OXFORD ENGLISH
are trade marks of Oxford University Press

ISBN 0 19 437207 3

Set by Wyvern Typesetting, Bristol
Printed in Hong Kong

for Maryann

Contents

Preface

Purpose

What justification might there be for a series of introductions to language study? After all, linguistics is already well served with introductory texts: expositions and explanations which are comprehensive and authoritative and excellent in their way. Generally speaking, however, their way is the essentially academic one of providing a detailed initiation into the discipline of linguistics, and they tend to be lengthy and technical: appropriately so, given their purpose. But they can be quite daunting to the novice. There is also a need for a more general and gradual introduction to language: transitional texts which will ease people into an understanding of complex ideas. This series of introductions is designed to serve this need.

Their purpose, therefore, is not to supplant but to support the more academically oriented introductions to linguistics: to prepare the conceptual ground. They are based on the belief that it is an advantage to have a broad map of the terrain sketched out before one considers its more specific features on a smaller scale, a general context in reference to which the detail makes sense. It is sometimes the case that students are introduced to detail without it being made clear what it is a detail *of*. Clearly, a general understanding of ideas is not sufficient: there needs to be closer scrutiny. But equally, close scrutiny can be myopic and meaningless unless it is related to the larger view. Indeed, it can be said that the precondition of more particular enquiry is an awareness of what, in general, the particulars are about. This series is designed to provide this large-scale view of different areas of language study. As such it can serve as a preliminary to (and precondition for) the more specific and specialized enquiry which students of linguistics are required to undertake.

But the series is not only intended to be helpful to such students. There are many people who take an interest in language without being academically engaged in linguistics *per se*. Such people may recognize the importance of understanding language for their own lines of enquiry, or for their own practical purposes, or quite simply for making them aware of something which figures so centrally in their everyday lives. If linguistics has revealing and relevant things to say about language, then this should presumably not be a privileged revelation, but one accessible to people other than linguists. These books have been so designed as to accommodate these broader interests too: they are meant to be introductions to language more generally as well as to linguistics as a discipline.

Design

The books in the series are all cut to the same basic pattern. There are four parts: Survey, Readings, References, and Glossary.

Survey

This is a summary overview of the main features of the area of language study concerned: its scope and principles of enquiry, its basic concerns and key concepts. These are expressed and explained in ways which are intended to make them as accessible as possible to people who have no prior knowledge or expertise in the subject. The Survey is written to be readable and is uncluttered by the customary scholarly references. In this sense, it is simple. But it is not simplistic. Lack of specialist expertise does not imply an inability to understand or evaluate ideas. Ignorance means lack of knowledge, not lack of intelligence. The Survey, therefore, is meant to be challenging. It draws a map of the subject area in such a way as to stimulate thought, and to invite a critical participation in the exploration of ideas. This kind of conceptual cartography has its dangers of course: the selection of what is significant, and the manner of its representation will not be to the liking of everybody, particularly not, perhaps, to some of those inside the discipline. But these surveys are written in the belief that there must be an alternative to a technical account on the one hand and an idiot's guide on the other if linguistics is to be made relevant to people in the wider world.

Readings

Some people will be content to read, and perhaps re read, the summary Survey. Others will want to pursue the subject and so will use the Survey as the preliminary for more detailed study. The Readings provide the necessary transition. For here the reader is presented with texts extracted from the specialist literature. The purpose of these readings is quite different from the Survey. It is to get readers to focus on the specifics of what is said and how it is said in these source texts. Questions are provided to further this purpose: they are designed to direct attention to points in each text, how they compare across texts, and how they deal with the issues discussed in the survey. The idea is to give readers an initial familiarity with the more specialist idiom of the linguistics literature, where the issues might not be so readily accessible, and to encourage them into close critical reading.

References

One way of moving into more detailed study is through the Readings. Another is through the annotated References in the third section of each book. Here there is a selection of works (books and articles) for further reading. Accompanying comments indicate how these deal in more detail with the issues discussed in the different chapters of the survey.

Glossary

Certain terms in the Survey appear in bold. These are terms used in a special or technical sense in the discipline. Their meanings are made clear in the discussion, but they are also explained in the Glossary at the end of each book. The Glossary is cross-referenced to the Survey, and therefore serves at the same time as an index. This enables readers to locate the term and what it signifies in the more general discussion, thereby, in effect, using the Survey as a summary work of reference.

Use

The series has been designed so as to be flexible in use. Each title is separate and self-contained, with only the basic format in common. The four sections of the format, as described here, can be drawn upon and combined in different ways, as required by the needs, or interests, of different readers. Some may be content with the Survey and the Glossary and may not want to follow up the suggested references. Some may not wish to venture into the Readings. Again, the Survey might be considered as appropriate preliminary reading for a course in applied linguistics or teacher education, and the Readings more appropriate for seminar discussion during the course. In short, the notion of an introduction will mean different things to different people, but in all cases the concern is to provide access to specialist knowledge and stimulate an awareness of its significance. This series as a whole has been designed to provide this access and promote this awareness in respect to different areas of language study.

H.G.WIDDOWSON

Survey

1
Definitions and background

Pragmatics is concerned with the study of meaning as communicated by a speaker (or writer) and interpreted by a listener (or reader). It has, consequently, more to do with the analysis of what people mean by their utterances than what the words or phrases in those utterances might mean by themselves. *Pragmatics is the study of speaker meaning.*

This type of study necessarily involves the interpretation of what people mean in a particular context and how the context influences what is said. It requires a consideration of how speakers organize what they want to say in accordance with who they're talking to, where, when, and under what circumstances. *Pragmatics is the study of contextual meaning.*

This approach also necessarily explores how listeners can make inferences about what is said in order to arrive at an interpretation of the speaker's intended meaning. This type of study explores how a great deal of what is unsaid is recognized as part of what is communicated. We might say that it is the investigation of invisible meaning. *Pragmatics is the study of how more gets communicated than is said.*

This perspective then raises the question of what determines the choice between the said and the unsaid. The basic answer is tied to the notion of distance. Closeness, whether it is physical, social, or conceptual, implies shared experience. On the assumption of how close or distant the listener is, speakers determine how much needs to be said. *Pragmatics is the study of the expression of relative distance.*

These are the four areas that pragmatics is concerned with. To understand how it got to be that way, we have to briefly review its relationship with other areas of linguistic analysis.

Syntax, semantics, and pragmatics

One traditional distinction in language analysis contrasts pragmatics with syntax and semantics. **Syntax** is the study of the relationships between linguistic forms, how they are arranged in sequence, and which sequences are well-formed. This type of study generally takes place without considering any world of reference or any user of the forms. **Semantics** is the study of the relationships between linguistic forms and entities in the world; that is, how words literally connect to things. Semantic analysis also attempts to establish the relationships between verbal descriptions and states of affairs in the world as accurate (true) or not, regardless of who produces that description.

Pragmatics is the study of the relationships between linguistic forms and the users of those forms. In this three-part distinction, only pragmatics allows humans into the analysis. The advantage of studying language via pragmatics is that one can talk about people's intended meanings, their assumptions, their purposes or goals, and the kinds of actions (for example, requests) that they are performing when they speak. The big disadvantage is that all these very human concepts are extremely difficult to analyze in a consistent and objective way. Two friends having a conversation may imply some things and infer some others without providing any clear linguistic evidence that we can point to as the explicit source of 'the meaning' of what was communicated. Example [1] is just such a problematic case. I heard the speakers, I knew what they said, but I had no idea what was communicated.

> [1] Her: So—did you?
>   Him: Hey—who wouldn't?

Thus, pragmatics is appealing because it's about how people make sense of each other linguistically, but it can be a frustrating area of study because it requires us to make sense of people and what they have in mind.

Regularity

Luckily, people tend to behave in fairly regular ways when it comes to using language. Some of that regularity derives from the fact that people are members of social groups and follow general patterns of behaviour expected within the group. Within a familiar social group, we normally find it easy to be polite and say appropriate things. In a new, unfamiliar social setting, we are often unsure about what to say and worry that we might say the wrong thing.

When I first lived in Saudi Arabia, I tended to answer questions in Arabic about my health (the equivalent of 'How are you?') with the equivalent of my familiar routine responses of 'Okay' or 'Fine'. However, I eventually noticed that when I asked a similar question, people generally answered with a phrase that had the literal meaning of 'Praise to God'. I soon learned to use the new expression, wanting to be pragmatically appropriate in that context. My first type of answer wasn't 'wrong' (my vocabulary and pronunciation weren't inaccurate), but it did convey the meaning that I was a social outsider who answered in an unexpected way. In other words, more was being communicated than was being said. Initially I did not know that: I had learned some linguistic forms in the language without learning the pragmatics of how those forms are used in a regular pattern by social insiders.

Another source of regularity in language use derives from the fact that most people within a linguistic community have similar basic experiences of the world and share a lot of non-linguistic knowledge. Let's say that, in the middle of a conversation, I mention the information in [2].

> [2] I found an old bicycle lying on the ground. The chain was rusted and the tires were flat.

You are unlikely to ask why a chain and some tires were suddenly being mentioned. I can normally assume that you will make the inference that if X is a bicycle, then X has a chain and tires (and many other regular parts). Because of this type of assumption, it would be pragmatically odd for me to have expressed [2] as [3].

> [3] I found an old bicycle. A bicycle has a chain. The chain was rusted. A bicycle also has tires. The tires were flat.

You would perhaps think that more was being communicated than was being said and that you were being treated as someone with no basic knowledge (i.e. as stupid). Once again, nothing in the use of the linguistic forms is inaccurate, but getting the pragmatics wrong might be offensive.

The types of regularities just described are extremely simple examples of language in use which are largely ignored by most linguistic analyses. To understand why it has become the province of pragmatics to investigate these, and many other, aspects of ordinary language in use, we need to take a brief historical look at how things got to be the way they are.

The pragmatics wastebasket

For a long period in the study of language, there has been a very strong interest in formal systems of analysis, often derived from mathematics and logic. The emphasis has been on discovering some of the abstract principles that lie at the very core of language. By placing the investigation of the abstract, potentially universal, features of language in the center of their work tables, linguists and philosophers of language tended to push any notes they had on everyday language use to the edges. As the tables got crowded, many of those notes on ordinary language in use began to be knocked off and ended up in the wastebasket. That overflowing wastebasket has become the source of much of what will be discussed in the following pages. It is worth remembering that the contents of that wastebasket were not originally organized under a single category. They were defined negatively, as the stuff that wasn't easily handled within the formal systems of analysis. Consequently, in order to understand some of the material that we're going to pull out of the wastebasket, we really have to look at how it got there.

The tables upon which many linguists and philosophers of language worked were devoted to the analysis of language structure. Consider the sentence in [4].

[4] The duck ran up to Mary and licked her.

A syntactic approach to this sentence would be concerned with the rules that determine the correct structure and exclude any incorrect orderings such as *'Up duck Mary to the ran'. Syntactic analysis would also be required to show that there is a missing element ('and _ licked her') before the verb 'licked' and to explicate the rules that allow that empty slot, or accept the pronoun 'it' in that position. However, those working on syntax would have thought it totally irrelevant if you tried to say that ducks don't do that and maybe the speaker had meant to say 'dog'. Indeed, from a purely syntactic perspective, a sentence like 'The bottle of ketchup ran up to Mary' is just as well-formed as [4].

Over on the semantics side of the table, however, there would have been concern. An entity labelled 'duck' has a meaning feature (animate) whereas a 'bottle of ketchup' would be (non-animate). Since a verb like 'ran up to' requires something animate as its subject, the word 'duck' is okay, but not a 'bottle of ketchup'.

Semantics is also concerned with the truth-conditions of propositions expressed in sentences. These propositions generally correspond to the basic literal meaning of a simple clause and are conventionally represented by the letters p, q, and r. Let's say that the underlying meaning relationship being expressed in 'The duck ran up to Mary' is the proposition p, and in 'the duck licked Mary', it is the proposition q. These two propositions are joined by the logical connector symbol for conjunction, & (called 'ampersand'). Thus, the propositional representation of the sentence in [4] is as in [5].

[5] $p \,\&\, q$

If p is true and q is true, then $p \,\&\, q$ is true. If either p or q is not true (i.e. false), then the conjunction of $p \,\&\, q$ is necessarily false. This type of analysis is used extensively in formal semantics.

Unfortunately, in this type of analysis, whenever $p \,\&\, q$ is true, it logically follows that $q \,\&\, p$ is true. Notice that $q \,\&\, p$, in this particular case, would have to be expressed as in [6].

[6] The duck licked Mary and ran up to her.

In the everyday world of language use, this state of affairs is not identical to the original situation described in [4]. There is a sequence of two events being described and we expect that sequence, in terms of occurrence, to be reflected in the order of mention.

If p involves some action and q involves another action, we have an overwhelming tendency to interpret the conjunction 'and', not as logical &, but as the sequential expression 'and then'. This is another example of more being communicated than is said. We might propose that there is a regular principle of language use which can be stated as in [7].

[7] Interpret order of mention as a reflection of order of occurrence.

What is expressed in [7] is not a rule of syntax or semantics. It isn't a rule at all. It is a pragmatic principle which we frequently use to make sense of what we hear and read, but which we can ignore if it doesn't apply in some situations.

There are many other principles of this type which will be explored in the following chapters. In Chapter 2, we will start with a really simple principle: the more two speakers have in common, the less language they'll need to use to identify familiar things. This principle accounts for the frequent use of words like 'this' and 'that' to refer to things in a shared physical context (for example, 'Would you like this or that?'). Exploring this basic aspect of language in use is the study of deixis.

2

Deixis and distance

Deixis is a technical term (from Greek) for one of the most basic things we do with utterances. It means 'pointing' via language. Any linguistic form used to accomplish this 'pointing' is called a **deictic expression**. When you notice a strange object and ask, 'What's that?', you are using a deictic expression ('that') to indicate something in the immediate context. Deictic expressions are also sometimes called **indexicals**. They are among the first forms to be spoken by very young children and can be used to indicate people via **person deixis** ('me', 'you'), or location via **spatial deixis** ('here', 'there'), or time via **temporal deixis** ('now', 'then'). All these expressions depend, for their interpretation, on the speaker and hearer sharing the same context. Indeed, deictic expressions have their most basic uses in face-to-face spoken interaction where utterances such as [1] are easily understood by the people present, but may need a translation for someone not right there.

[1] I'll put this here.

(Of course, you understood that Jim was telling Anne that he was about to put an extra house key in one of the kitchen drawers.)

Deixis is clearly a form of referring that is tied to the speaker's context, with the most basic distinction between deictic expressions being 'near speaker' versus 'away from speaker'. In English, the 'near speaker', or **proximal** terms, are 'this', 'here', 'now'. The 'away from speaker', or **distal** terms, are 'that', 'there', 'then'. Proximal terms are typically interpreted in terms of the speaker's location, or the **deictic center**, so that 'now' is generally understood as referring to some point or period in time that has the time of the speaker's utterance at its center. Distal terms can simply indicate 'away from speaker', but, in some languages, can be used to distinguish between 'near addressee' and 'away from both speaker and addressee'. Thus, in Japanese, the translation of the pronoun 'that' will distinguish between 'that near addressee' '*sore*' and 'that distant from both speaker and addressee' '*are*' with a third term being used for the proximal 'this near speaker' '*kore*'.

Person deixis

The distinction just described involves person deixis, with the speaker ('I') and the addressee ('you') mentioned. The simplicity of these forms disguises the complexity of their use. To learn these deictic expressions, we have to discover that each person in a conversation shifts from being 'I' to being 'you' constantly. All young children go through a stage in their learning where this distinction seems problematic and they say things like 'Read you a story' (instead of 'me') when handing over a favorite book.

Person deixis clearly operates on a basic three-part division, exemplified by the pronouns for first person ('I'), second person ('you'), and third person ('he', 'she', or 'it'). In many languages these deictic categories of speaker, addressee, and other(s) are elaborated with markers of relative social status (for example, addressee with higher status versus addressee with lower status). Expressions which indicate higher status are described as **honorifics**. The discussion of the circumstances which lead to the choice of one of these forms rather than another is sometimes described as **social deixis.**

A fairly well-known example of a social contrast encoded within person deixis is the distinction between forms used for a familiar versus a non-familiar addressee in some languages. This is known as the **T/V distinction**, from the French forms '*tu*' (familiar) and '*vous*' (non-familiar), and is found in many languages including German ('*du/Sie*') and Spanish ('*tú/Usted*'). The choice of one form will certainly communicate something (not directly said) about the speaker's view of his or her relationship with the addressee. In those social contexts where individuals typically mark distinctions between the social status of the speaker and addressee, the higher, older, and more powerful speaker will tend to use the *'tu'* version to a lower, younger, and less powerful addressee, and be addressed by the *'vous'* form in return. When social change is taking place, as for example in modern Spain, where a young businesswoman (higher economic status) is talking to her older cleaning lady (lower economic status), how do they address each other? I am told that the age distinction remains more powerful than the economic distinction and the older woman uses *'tú'* and the younger uses *'Usted'*.

The Spanish non-familiar version (*'Usted'*) is historically related to a form which was used to refer to neither first person (speaker) nor second person (addressee), but to third person (some other). In deictic terms, third person is not a direct participant in basic (I–you) interaction and, being an outsider, is necessarily more distant. Third person pronouns are consequently distal forms in terms of person deixis. Using a third person form, where a second person form would be possible, is one way of communicating distance (and non-familiarity). This can be done in English for an ironic or humorous purpose as when one person, who's very busy in the kitchen, addresses another, who's being very lazy, as in [2].

[2] Would his highness like some coffee?

The distance associated with third person forms is also used to make potential accusations (for example, 'you didn't clean up') less direct, as in [3a.], or to make a potentially personal issue seem like an impersonal one, based on a general rule, as in [3b.].

[3] a. Somebody didn't clean up after himself.
     b. Each person has to clean up after him or herself.

Of course, the speaker can state such general 'rules' as applying to the speaker plus other(s), by using the first person plural ('we'), as in [4].

[4] We clean up after ourselves around here.

There is, in English, a potential ambiguity in such uses which allows two different interpretations. There is an **exclusive 'we'** (speaker plus other(s), excluding addressee) and an **inclusive 'we'** (speaker and addressee included). Some languages grammaticize this distinction (for example, Fijian has *'keimami'* for exclusive first person plural and *'keda'* for inclusive first person plural).

In English, the ambiguity present in [4] provides a subtle opportunity for a hearer to decide what was communicated. Either the hearer decides that he or she is a member of the group to whom the rule applies (i.e. an addressee) or an outsider to whom the rule does not apply (i.e. not an addressee). In this case the hearer gets to decide the kind of 'more' that is being communicated.

The inclusive–exclusive distinction may also be noted in the difference between saying 'Let's go' (to some friends) and 'Let us go' (to someone who has captured the speaker and friends). The action of going is inclusive in the first, but exclusive in the second.

Spatial deixis

The concept of distance already mentioned is clearly relevant to spatial deixis, where the relative location of people and things is being indicated. Contemporary English makes use of only two adverbs, 'here' and 'there', for the basic distinction, but in older texts and in some dialects, a much larger set of deictic expressions can be found. Although 'yonder' (more distant from speaker) is still used, words like 'hither' (to this place) and 'thence' (from that place) now sound archaic. These last two adverbs include the meaning of motion toward or away from the speaker. Some verbs of motion, such as 'come' and 'go', retain a deictic sense when they are used to mark movement toward the speaker ('Come to bed!') or away from the speaker ('Go to bed!').

One version of the concept of motion toward speaker (i.e. becoming visible), seems to be the first deictic meaning learned by children and characterizes their use of words like 'this' and 'here' (= can be seen). They are distinct from 'that' and 'there' which are associated with things that move out of the child's visual space (= can no longer be seen).

In considering spatial deixis, however, it is important to remember that location from the speaker's perspective can be fixed mentally as well as physically. Speakers temporarily away from their home location will often continue to use 'here' to mean the (physically distant) home location, as if they were still in that location. Speakers also seem to be able to project themselves into other locations prior to actually being in those locations, as when they say 'I'll come later' (= movement to addressee's location).

This is sometimes described as **deictic projection** and we make more use of its possibilities as more technology allows us to manipulate location. If 'here' means the place of the speaker's utterance (and 'now' means the time of the speaker's utterance), then an utterance such as [5] should be nonsense.

[5] I am not here now.

However, I can say [5] into the recorder of a telephone answering machine, projecting that the 'now' will apply to any time some-one tries to call me, and not to when I actually record the words. Indeed, recording [5] is a kind of dramatic per-formance for a future audience in which I project my presence to be in the required location. A similar deictic projection is accom-plished via dramatic performance when I use direct speech to represent the person, location, and feelings of someone or some-thing else. For example, I could be telling you about a visit to a pet store, as in [6].

[6] I was looking at this little puppy in a cage with such a sad look on its face. It was like, 'Oh, I'm so unhappy here, will you set me free?'

The 'here' of the cage is not the actual physical location of the person uttering the words (the speaker), but is instead the loca-tion of that person performing in the role of the puppy.

It may be that the truly pragmatic basis of spatial deixis is actu-ally **psychological distance**. Physically close objects will tend to be treated by the speaker as psychologically close. Also, something that is physically distant will generally be treated as psycho-logically distant (for example, 'that man over there'). However, a speaker may also wish to mark something that is physically close (for example, a perfume being sniffed by the speaker) as psycho-logically distant 'I don't like that'. In this analysis, a word like 'that' does not have a fixed (i.e. semantic) meaning; instead, it is 'invested' with meaning in a context by a speaker.

Similar psychological processes seem to be at work in our dis-tinctions between proximal and distal expressions used to mark temporal deixis.

Temporal deixis

We have already noted the use of the proximal form 'now' as indicating both the time coinciding with the speaker's utterance and the time of the speaker's voice being heard (the hearer's 'now'). In contrast to 'now', the distal expression 'then' applies to both past [7a.] and future [7b.] time relative to the speaker's present time.

[7] a. November 22nd, 1963? I was in Scotland then.
    b. Dinner at 8:30 on Saturday? Okay, I'll see you then.

It is worth noting that we also use elaborate systems of non-deictic temporal reference such as calendar time (dates, as in [7a.]) and clock time (hours, as in [7b.]). However, these forms of temporal reference are learned a lot later than the deictic expressions like 'yesterday', 'tomorrow', 'today', 'tonight', 'next week', 'last week', 'this week'. All these expressions depend for their interpretation on knowing the relevant utterance time. If we don't know the utterance (i.e. scribbling) time of a note, as in [8], on an office door, we won't know if we have a short or a long wait ahead.

[8] Back in an hour.

Similarly, if we return the next day to a bar that displays the notice in [9], then we will still be (deictically) one day early for the free drink.

[9] Free Beer Tomorrow.

The psychological basis of temporal deixis seems to be similar to that of spatial deixis. We can treat temporal events as objects that move toward us (into view) or away from us (out of view). One metaphor used in English is of events coming toward the speaker from the future (for example, 'the coming week', 'the approaching year') and going away from the speaker to the past (for example, 'in days gone by', 'the past week'). We also seem to treat the near or immediate future as being close to utterance time by using the proximal deictic 'this', as in 'this (coming) weekend' or 'this (coming) Thursday'.

One basic (but often unrecognized) type of temporal deixis in English is in the choice of verb tense. Whereas other languages have many different forms of the verb as different tenses, English has only two basic forms, the present as in [10a.], and the past as in [10b.].

[10] a. I live here now.
b. I lived there then.

The present tense is the proximal form and the past tense is the distal form. Something having taken place in the past, as in [11a.], is typically treated as distant from the speaker's current situation. Perhaps less obviously, something that is treated as extremely unlikely (or impossible) from the speaker's current situation is also marked via the distal (past tense) form, as in [11b.].

[11] a. I could swim (when I was a child).
b. I could be in Hawaii (if I had a lot of money).

The past tense is always used in English in those *if*-clauses that mark events presented by the speaker as not being close to present reality as in [12].

[12] a. If I had a yacht, …
b. If I was rich, …

Neither of the ideas expressed in [12] are to be treated as having happened in past time. They are presented as deictically distant from the speaker's current situation. So distant, indeed, that they actually communicate the negative (we infer that the speaker has no yacht and is not rich).

In order to understand many English conditional constructions (including those of the form 'Had I known sooner …'), we have to recognize that, in temporal deixis, the remote or distal form can be used to communicate not only distance from current time, but also distance from current reality or facts.

Deixis and grammar

The basic distinctions presented so far for person, spatial, and temporal deixis can all be seen at work in one of the most common structural distinctions made in English grammar—that between direct and indirect (or reported) speech. As already described, the deictic expressions for person ('you'), place ('here'), and time ('this evening') can all be interpreted within the same context as the speaker who utters [13a.].

[13] a. Are you planning to be here this evening?
 b. I asked her if she was planning to be there that
 evening.

When the context shifts, as for example in [13b.], to one in which I report the previous utterance, then the previous utterance is marked deictically as relative to the circumstances of asking. Note that the proximal forms presented in [13a.] have shifted to the corresponding distal forms in [13b.]. This very regular difference in English reported discourse marks a distinction between the 'near speaker' meaning of direct speech and the 'away from speaker' meaning of indirect speech. The proximal deictic forms of a direct speech reporting communicate, often dramatically, a sense of being in the same context as the utterance. The distal deictic forms of indirect speech reporting make the original speech event seem more remote.

It should not be a surprise to learn that deictic expressions were all to be found in the pragmatics wastebasket. Their interpretation depends on the context, the speaker's intention, and they express relative distance. Given their small size and extremely wide range of possible uses, deictic expressions always communicate much more than is said.

3
Reference and inference

Throughout the preceding discussion of deixis, there was an assumption that the use of words to refer to people and things was a relatively straightforward matter. It is indeed fairly easy for people to do, but it is rather difficult to explain how they do it. We do know that words themselves don't refer to anything. People refer. We might best think of **reference** as an act in which a speaker, or writer, uses linguistic forms to enable a listener, or reader, to identify something.

Those linguistic forms are **referring expressions**, which can be proper nouns (for example, 'Shakespeare', 'Cathy Revuelto', 'Hawaii'), noun phrases which are definite (for example, 'the author', 'the singer', 'the island'), or indefinite (for example, 'a man', 'a woman', 'a beautiful place'), and pronouns (for example, 'he', 'her', 'it', 'them'). The choice of one type of referring expression rather than another seems to be based, to a large extent, on what the speaker assumes the listener already knows. In shared visual contexts, those pronouns that function as deictic expressions (for example, 'Take this'; 'Look at him!') may be sufficient for successful reference, but where identification seems more difficult, more elaborate noun phrases may be used (for example, 'Remember the old foreign guy with the funny hat?').

Reference, then, is clearly tied to the speaker's goals (for example, to identify something) and the speaker's beliefs (i.e. can the listener be expected to know that particular something?) in the use of language. For successful reference to occur, we must also recognize the role of **inference**. Because there is no direct relationship between entities and words, the listener's task is to infer correctly which entity the speaker intends to identify by using a particular referring expression. It is not unusual for people to want to refer to some entity or person without knowing exactly which 'name' would be the best word to use. We can even use vague expressions (for example, 'the blue thing', 'that icky stuff', 'ol' what's his name', 'the thingamajig'), relying on the listener's ability to infer what referent we have in mind. Speakers even invent names. There was one man who delivered packages to our office whose 'real' name I didn't know, but whose identity I could infer when the secretary referred to him as in [1].

[1] Mister Aftershave is late today.

The example in [1] may serve to illustrate that reference is not based on an objectively correct (versus incorrect) naming, but on some locally successful (versus unsuccessful) choice of expression.

We might also note from example [1] that successful reference is necessarily collaborative, with both the speaker and the listener having a role in thinking about what the other has in mind.

Referential and attributive uses

It is important to recognize that not all referring expressions have identifiable physical referents. Indefinite noun phrases can be used to identify a physically present entity as in [2a.], but they can also be used to describe entities that are assumed to exist, but are unknown, as in [2b.], or entities that, as far as we know, don't exist [2c.].

[2] a. There's a man waiting for you.
b. He wants to marry a woman with lots of money.
c. We'd love to find a nine-foot-tall basketball player.

The expression in [2b.], 'a woman with lots of money', can designate an entity that is known to the speaker only in terms of its descriptive properties. The word 'a' could be replaced by 'any' in this case. This is sometimes called an **attributive use**, meaning 'whoever/whatever fits the description'. It would be distinct from a **referential use** whereby I actually have a person in mind and, instead of using her name or some other description, I choose the expression in [2b.], perhaps because I think you'd be more interested in hearing that this woman has lots of money than that she has a name.

A similar distinction can be found with definite noun phrases. During a news report on a mysterious death, the reporter may say [3] without knowing for sure if there is a person who could be the referent of the definite expression 'the killer'. This would be an attributive use (i.e. 'whoever did the killing'), based on the speaker's assumption that a referent must exist.

[3] There was no sign of the killer.

However, if a particular individual had been identified as having done the killing and had been chased into a building, but escaped, then uttering the sentence in [3] about that individual would be a referential use, based on the speaker's knowledge that a referent does exist.

The point of this distinction is that expressions themselves cannot be treated as having reference (as is often assumed in semantic treatments), but are, or are not, 'invested' with referential function in a context by a speaker or writer. Speakers often invite us to assume, via attributive uses, that we can identify what they're talking about, even when the entity or individual described may not exist, as in [2c.]. Some other famous members of that group are the tooth fairy and Santa Claus.

Names and referents

The version of reference being presented here is one in which there is a basic 'intention-to-identify' and a 'recognition-of-intention' collaboration at work. This process need not only work between one speaker and one listener; it appears to work, in terms of convention, between all members of a community who share a common language and culture. That is, there is a convention that certain referring expressions will be used to identify certain entities on a regular basis. It is our daily experience of the successful operation of this convention that may cause us to assume that referring expressions can only designate very specific entities. This assumption may lead us to think that a name or proper noun like 'Shakespeare' can only be used to identify one specific person, and an expression containing a common noun, such as 'the cheese sandwich', can only be used to identify a specific thing. This belief is mistaken. A truly pragmatic view of reference allows us to see how a person can be identified via the expression, 'the cheese sandwich', and a thing can be identified via the name, 'Shakespeare'.

For example, it would not be strange for one student to ask another the question in [4a.] and receive the reply in [4b.].

[4] a. Can I borrow your Shakespeare?
  b. Yeah, it's over there on the table.

Given the context just created, the intended referent and the inferred referent would not be a person, but probably a book (notice the pronoun 'it').

In a restaurant, one waiter brings out an order of food for another waiter and asks him [5a.] and hears [5b.] in reply.

[5] a. Where's the cheese sandwich sitting?
  b. He's over there by the window.

Given the context, the referent being identified is not a thing, but a person (notice the pronoun 'he').

The examples in [4] and [5] may allow us to see more clearly how reference actually works. The Shakespeare example in [4] suggests that there is a conventional (and potentially culture-specific) set of entities that can be identifed by the use of a writer's name. Let us call them 'things the writer produced'. This would allow us to make sense of the sentences in [6].

[6] a. Shakespeare takes up the whole bottom shelf.
  b. We're going to see Shakespeare in London.
  c. I hated Shakespeare at school.

Obviously, this convention does not only apply to writers, but also to artists [7a.], composers [7b.], musicians [7c.], and many other producers of objects.

[7] a. Picasso's on the far wall.
  b. The new Mozart is better value than the Bach.
  c. My Rolling Stones is missing.

There appears to be a **pragmatic connection** between proper names and objects that will be conventionally associated, within a socio-culturally defined community, with those names. Using a proper name referentially to identify any such object invites the listener to make the expected inference (for example, from name of writer to book by writer) and thereby show himself or herself to be a member of the same community as the speaker. In such cases, it is rather obvious that more is being communicated than is said.

The nature of reference interpretation just described is also what allows readers to make sense of newspaper headlines using names of countries, as exemplified in [8a.] where the referent is to be understood as a soccer team, not as a government, and in [8b.] where it is to be understood as a government, not as a soccer team.

[8] a. Brazil wins World Cup.
   b. Japan wins first round of trade talks.

The role of co-text

In many of the preceding examples, our ability to identify intended referents has actually depended on more than our understanding of the referring expression. It has been aided by the linguistic material, or **co-text**, accompanying the referring expression. When [8a.] appeared as a headline, 'Brazil' was a referring expression and 'wins World Cup' was part of the co-text (the rest of the newspaper was more co-text). The co-text clearly limits the range of possible interpretations we might have for a word like 'Brazil'. It is consequently misleading to think of reference being understood solely in terms of our ability to identify referents via the referring expression. The referring expression actually provides a **range of reference**, that is, a number of possible referents. Returning to a previous example, we can show that, while the phrase 'the cheese sandwich' stays the same, the different co-texts in [9a.] and [9b.] lead to a different type of interpretation in each case (i.e. 'food' in [9a.] and 'person' in [9b.]).

[9] a. The cheese sandwich is made with white bread.
   b. The cheese sandwich left without paying.

Of course, co-text is just a linguistic part of the environment in which a referring expression is used. The physical environment, or **context**, is perhaps more easily recognized as having a powerful impact on how referring expressions are to be interpreted. The physical context of a restaurant, and perhaps even the speech conventions of those who work there, may be crucial to the interpretation of [9b.]. Similarly, it is useful to know that a hospital is the context for [10a.], a dentist's office for [10b.], and a hotel reception for [10c.].

> [10] a. The heart-attack mustn't be moved.
> b. Your ten-thirty just cancelled.
> c. A couple of rooms have complained about the heat.

The examples in [10] provide some support for an analysis of reference that depends on local context and the local knowledge of the participants. It may crucially depend on familiarity with the local socio-cultural conventions as the basis for inference (for example, if a person is in a hospital with an illness, then he or she can be identified by nurses via the name of the illness). These conventions may differ substantially from one social group to another and may be marked differently from one language to another. Reference, then, is not simply a relationship between the meaning of a word or phrase and an object or person in the world. It is a social act, in which the speaker assumes that the word or phrase chosen to identify an object or person will be interpreted as the speaker intended.

Anaphoric reference

The preceding discussion has been concerned with single acts of reference. In most of our talk and writing, however, we have to keep track of who or what we are talking about for more than one sentence at a time. After the initial introduction of some entity, speakers will use various expressions to maintain reference, as in [11].

> [11] In the film, a man and a woman were trying to wash a cat. The man was holding the cat while the woman poured water on it. He said something to her and they started laughing.

In English, initial reference, or introductory mention, is often indefinite ('a man', 'a woman', 'a cat'). In [11] the definite noun phrases ('the man', 'the cat', 'the woman') and the pronouns ('it', 'he', 'her', 'they') are examples of subsequent reference to already introduced referents, generally known as anaphoric reference, or anaphora. In technical terms, the second or subsequent expression is the **anaphor** and the initial expression is the **antecedent**.

It is tempting to think of anaphoric reference as a process of continuing to identify exactly the same entity as denoted by the antecedent. In many cases, that assumption makes little difference to the interpretation, but in those cases where some change or effect is described, the anaphoric reference must be interpreted differently. In example [12], from a recipe, the initial referring expression 'six potatoes' identifies something different from the anaphoric pronoun 'them' which must be interpreted as 'the six peeled and sliced potatoes'.

[12] Peel and slice six potatoes. Put them in cold salted water.

There is also a reversal of the antecedent–anaphor pattern sometimes found at the beginning of stories, as in example [13].

[13] I turned the corner and almost stepped on it. There was a large snake in the middle of the path.

Note that the pronoun 'it' is used first and is difficult to interpret until the full noun phrase is presented in the next line. This pattern is technically known as **cataphora**, and is much less common than anaphora.

There is a range of expressions which are used for anaphoric reference in English. The most typical forms are pronouns, such as 'it' in [14a.], but definite noun phrases are also used, for example, 'the slices' in [14b.].

[14] a. Peel an onion and slice it.
    b. Drop the slices into hot oil.
    c. Cook for three minutes.

When the interpretation requires us to identify an entity, as in 'Cook (?) for three minutes', in [14c.], and no linguistic expression is present, it is called **zero anaphora**, or **ellipsis**. The use of zero anaphora as a means of maintaining reference clearly creates an expectation that the listener will be able to infer who or what the speaker intends to identify. It is also another obvious case of more being communicated than is said.

The listener is also expected to make more specific types of inference when the anaphoric expressions don't seem to be linguistically connected to their antecedents. This point was noted in

Chapter 1 with the 'bicycle' example, and is further illustrated in [15].

[15] a. I just rented a house. The kitchen is really big.
       b. We had Chardonnay with dinner. The wine was the best part.
       c. The bus came on time, but he didn't stop.

Making sense of [15a.] requires an inference (i.e. if x is a house, then x has a kitchen) to make the anaphoric connection. Such inferences depend on assumed knowledge which, as in [15b.], may be much more specific (i.e. Chardonnay is a kind of wine). In addition, the inference can be considered so automatic for some speakers (for example, a bus has a driver), that they can go straight to a pronoun for anaphoric reference, as in [15c.]. In this example, note that the antecedent ('the bus') and the anaphor ('he') are not in grammatical agreement (i.e. normally a bus would be 'it'). As pointed out already, successful reference does not depend on some strictly literal, or grammatically 'correct', relationship between the properties of the referent and the referring expression chosen. The word 'sandwich' can identify a person and the pronoun 'he' can be an anaphor for a thing. The key to making sense of reference is that pragmatic process whereby speakers select linguistic expressions with the intention of identifying certain entities and with the assumption that listeners will collaborate and interpret those expressions as the speaker intended.

The social dimension of reference may also be tied to the effect of collaboration. The immediate recognition of an intended referent, even when a minimal referring expression (for example, a pronoun) is used, represents something shared, something in common, and hence social closeness. Successful reference means that an intention was recognized, via inference, indicating a kind of shared knowledge and hence social connection. The assumption of shared knowledge is also crucially involved in the study of presupposition.

4
Presupposition and entailment

In the preceding discussion of reference, there was an appeal to the idea that speakers assume certain information is already known by their listeners. Because it is treated as known, such information will generally not be stated and consequently will count as part of what is communicated but not said. The technical terms presupposition and entailment are used to describe two different aspects of this kind of information.

It is worth noting at the outset that presupposition and entailment were considered to be much more central to pragmatics in the past than they are now. In more recent approaches, there has been less interest in the type of technical discussion associated with the logical analysis of these phenomena. Without some introduction to that type of analytic discussion, however, it becomes very difficult to understand how the current relationship between semantics and pragmatics developed. Much of what follows in this chapter is designed to illustrate the process of thinking through a number of problems in the analysis of some aspects of invisible meaning. Let's begin by defining our terms.

A **presupposition** is something the speaker assumes to be the case prior to making an utterance. Speakers, not sentences, have presuppositions. An **entailment** is something that logically follows from what is asserted in the utterance. Sentences, not speakers, have entailments.

We can identify some of the potentially assumed information that would be associated with the utterance of [1].

[1] Mary's brother bought three horses.

In producing the utterance in [1], the speaker will normally be expected to have the presuppositions that a person called Mary exists and that she has a brother. The speaker may also hold the more specific presuppositions that Mary has only one brother and that he has a lot of money. All of these presuppositions are the speaker's and all of them can be wrong, in fact. The sentence in [1] will be treated as having the entailments that Mary's brother bought something, bought three animals, bought two horses, bought one horse, and many other similar logical consequences. These entailments follow from the sentence, regardless of whether the speaker's beliefs are right or wrong, in fact. They are communicated without being said. Because of its logical nature, however, entailment is not generally discussed as much in contemporary pragmatics as the more speaker-dependent notion of presupposition.

Presupposition

In many discussions of the concept, presupposition is treated as a relationship between two propositions. If we say that the sentence in [2a.] contains the proposition p and the sentence in [2b.] contains the proposition q, then, using the symbol >> to mean 'presupposes', we can represent the relationship as in [2c.].

[2] a. Mary's dog is cute. $(= p)$
    b. Mary has a dog. $(= q)$
    c. $p >> q$

Interestingly, when we produce the opposite of the sentence in [2a.] by negating it $(= \text{NOT } p)$, as in [3a.], we find that the relationship of presupposition doesn't change. That is, the same proposition q, repeated as [3b.], continues to be presupposed by NOT p, as shown in [3c.].

[3] a. Mary's dog isn't cute. $(= \text{NOT } p)$
    b. Mary has a dog. $(= q)$
    c. NOT $p >> q$

This property of presupposition is generally described as **constancy under negation**. Basically, it means that the presupposition of a statement will remain constant (i.e. still true) even when that statement is negated. As a further example, consider a situation in which you disagree (via a negative, as in [4b.]) with someone who has already made the statement in [4a.].

[4] a. Everybody knows that John is gay.　　　　(= p)
　　b. Everybody doesn't know that John is gay.　(= NOT p)
　　c. John is gay.　　　　　　　　　　　　　　(= q)
　　d. $p \gg q$ & NOT $p \gg q$

Notice that, although both speakers disagree about the validity of p (i.e. the statement in [4a.]), they both assume the truth of q (i.e. [4c.]) in making their statements. The proposition q, as shown in [4d.], is presupposed by both p and NOT p, remaining constant under negation.

Types of presupposition

In the analysis of how speakers' assumptions are typically expressed, presupposition has been associated with the use of a large number of words, phrases, and structures. We shall consider these linguistic forms here as indicators of **potential presuppositions**, which can only become actual presuppositions in contexts with speakers.

As already illustrated in examples [1] to [3], the possessive construction in English is associated with a presupposition of existence. The **existential presupposition** is not only assumed to be present in possessive constructions (for example, 'your car' >> 'you have a car'), but more generally in any definite noun phrase. By using any of the expressions in [5], the speaker is assumed to be committed to the existence of the entities named.

[5] the King of Sweden, the cat, the girl next door,
　　the Counting Crows

We shall reconsider the basis of existential presuppositions later, but first we should note that there was a different type of presupposition present in [4]. In [4], the verb 'know' occurs in a structure, 'Everybody knows that q', with q as the presupposition. The presupposed information following a verb like 'know' can be treated as a fact, and is described as a **factive presupposition**. A number of other verbs, such as 'realize' in [6a.] and 'regret' in [6b.], as well as phrases involving 'be' with 'aware' [6c.], 'odd' [6d.], and 'glad' [6e.] have factive presuppositions.

[6] a. She didn't realize he was ill.   (>> He was ill)
    b. We regret telling him.   (>> We told him)
    c. I wasn't aware that she was
       married.   (>> She was married)
    d. It isn't odd that he left early.   (>> He left early)
    e. I'm glad that it's over.   (>> It's over)

There are also a number of other forms which may best be treated as the source of lexical presuppositions. Generally speaking, in **lexical presupposition**, the use of one form with its asserted meaning is conventionally interpreted with the presupposition that another (non-asserted) meaning is understood. Each time you say that someone 'managed' to do something, the asserted meaning is that the person succeeded in some way. When you say that someone 'didn't manage', the asserted meaning is that the person did not succeed. In both cases, however, there is a presupposition (non-asserted) that the person 'tried' to do that something. So, 'managed' is conventionally interpreted as *asserting* 'succeeded' and *presupposing* 'tried'. Other examples, involving the lexical items, 'stop', 'start', and 'again', are presented, with their presuppositions, in [7].

[7] a. He stopped smoking.   (>> He used to smoke)
    b. They started complaining.   (>> They weren't
       complaining before)
    c. You're late again.   (>> You were late before)

In the case of lexical presupposition, the speaker's use of a particular expression is taken to presuppose another (unstated) concept, whereas in the case of a factive presupposition, the use of a particular expression is taken to presuppose the truth of the information that is stated after it.

In addition to presuppositions which are associated with the use of certain words and phrases, there are also **structural presuppositions**. In this case, certain sentence structures have been analyzed as conventionally and regularly presupposing that part of the structure is already assumed to be true. We might say that speakers can use such structures to treat information as presupposed (i.e. assumed to be true) and hence to be accepted as true by the listener. For example, the *wh*-question construction in English, as shown in [8a.] and [8b.], is conventionally interpreted with the presupposition that the information after the *wh*-form (i.e. 'When' and 'Where') is already known to be the case.

[8] a. When did he leave? (>> He left)
b. Where did you buy the bike? (>> You bought the bike)

The type of presupposition illustrated in [8] can lead listeners to believe that the information presented is necessarily true, rather than just the presupposition of the person asking the question. For example, let's say that you were standing at an intersection one evening. You didn't notice whether the traffic signal had turned to red before a car went through the intersection. The car was immediately involved in a crash. You were witness to the crash and later you are asked the question in [9].

[9] How fast was the car going when it ran the red light?

If you answer the question as asked (Just answer the question!) and estimate the speed of the car, then you would appear to be accepting the truth of the presupposition (i.e. >> the car ran the red light). Such structurally-based presuppositions may represent subtle ways of making information that the speaker believes appear to be what the listener should believe.

So far, we have only considered contexts in which presuppositions are assumed to be true. There are, however, examples of non-factive presuppositions associated with a number of verbs in English. A **non-factive presupposition** is one that is assumed not to be true. Verbs like 'dream', 'imagine', and 'pretend', as shown in [10], are used with the presupposition that what follows is not true.

[10] a. I dreamed that I was rich. (>> I was not rich)
b. We imagined we were in Hawaii. (>> We were not in Hawaii)
c. He pretends to be ill. (>> He is not ill)

We have already noted, at the end of the discussion of deixis, a structure that is interpreted with a non-factive presupposition ('If I had a yacht, …'). Indeed, this type of structure creates a **counter-factual presupposition**, meaning that what is presupposed is not only not true, but is the opposite of what is true, or 'contrary to facts'. A conditional structure of the type shown in [11], generally called a counterfactual conditional, presupposes that the information in the *if*-clause is not true at the time of utterance.

[11] If you were my friend, you would have helped me.
(>> You are not my friend)

The existence of non-factive presuppositions is part of an interesting problem for the analysis of utterances with complex structures, generally known as 'the projection problem', to be explored in the next section.

Indicators of potential presuppositions discussed so far are summarized in Table 4.1.

Type	Example	Presupposition
existential	the X	>> X exists
factive	I regret leaving	>> I left
non-factive	He pretended to be happy	>> He wasn't happy
lexical	He managed to escape	>> He tried to escape
structural	When did she die?	>> She died
counterfactual	If I weren't ill,	>> I am ill

TABLE 4.1 *Potential presuppositions*

The projection problem

There is a basic expectation that the presupposition of a simple sentence will continue to be true when that simple sentence becomes part of a more complex sentence. This is one version of the general idea that the meaning of the whole sentence is a combination of the meaning of its parts. However, the meaning of some presuppositions (as 'parts') doesn't survive to become the meaning of some complex sentences (as 'wholes'). This is known as the **projection problem**. In example [12], we are going to see what happens to the presupposition q ('Kelly was ill') which is assumed to be true in the simple structure of [12c.], but which does not 'project' into the complex structure [12h.]. In order to follow this type of analysis, we have to think of a situation in which a person might say: 'I imagined that Kelly was ill and nobody realized that she was ill.'

[12] a. Nobody realized that Kelly was ill. $(= p)$
　　　 b. Kelly was ill. $(= q)$
　　　 c. $p >> q$

(At this point, the speaker uttering [12a.]
presupposes [12b.].)

  d. I imagined that Kelly was ill.   ($= r$)

  e. Kelly was not ill.   ($=$ NOT q)

  f. $r >>$ NOT q
(At this point, the speaker uttering [12d.]
presupposes [12e.], the opposite of [12b.].)

  g. I imagined that Kelly was ill and nobody
realized that she was ill.   ($= r \,\&\, p$)

  h. $r \,\&\, p >>$ NOT q
(At this point, after combining $r \,\&\, p$, the presupposition q can no longer be assumed to be true.)

In an example like [12], the technical analysis may be straight-forward, but it may be difficult to think of a context in which someone would talk like that. Perhaps example [13] will contextualize better. In an episode of a TV soap opera, two characters have the dialog in [13].

[13] William: It's so sad. Blaine regrets getting Gigi pregnant.
      Stan: But he didn't get her pregnant. We know that now.

If we combine two of the utterances from [13], we have the sequence, 'Blaine regrets getting Gigi pregnant; but he didn't get her pregnant'. Identifying the different propositions involved, as in [14], we can see that the presupposition q in [14b.] does not survive as a presupposition of the combined utterances in [14e.].

[14] a. Blaine regrets getting Gigi pregnant.   ($= p$)

    b. Blaine got Gigi pregnant.   ($= q$)

    c. $p >> q$

    d. He didn't get her pregnant.   ($= r$)

    e. Blaine regrets getting Gigi pregnant,
but he didn't get her pregnant.   ($= p \,\&\, r$)

    f. $p \,\&\, r >>$ NOT q

One way to think about the whole sentence presented in [14e.] is as an utterance by a person reporting what happened in the soap opera that day. That person will not assume the presupposition q (i.e. that Blaine got Gigi pregnant) is true when uttering [14e.].

A simple explanation for the fact that presuppositions don't 'project' is that they are destroyed by entailments. Remember that an entailment is something that necessarily follows from what is asserted. In example [13], Stan's utterance of 'he didn't get her pregnant' actually entails 'Blaine didn't get Gigi pregnant' as a logical consequence. Thus, when the person who watched the soap opera tells you that 'Blaine regrets getting Gigi pregnant, but he didn't get her pregnant', you have a presupposition q and an entailment NOT q. The entailment (a necessary consequence of what is said) is simply more powerful than the presupposition (an earlier assumption).

The power of entailment can also be used to cancel existential presuppositions. Normally we assume that when a person uses a definite description of the type 'the X' (for example, 'the King of England'), he or she presupposes the existence of the entity described, as in the utterance of [15a.]. Also, in any utterance of the form 'X doesn't exist', as in [15b.], there is an entailment that there is no X. But does the speaker of [15b.] also still have the presupposition of the existence of the entity described?

[15] a. The King of England visited us.
b. The King of England doesn't exist!

Instead of thinking that a speaker who utters [15b.] simultaneously believes that there is a King of England (= presupposition) and that there is not a King of England (= entailment), we recognize that the entailment is more powerful than the presupposition. We abandon the existential presupposition.

As already emphasized, it may be best to think of all the types of presuppositions illustrated in Table 4.1 as 'potential presuppositions' which only become actual presuppositions when intended by speakers to be recognized as such within utterances. Speakers can indeed indicate that the potential presupposition is not being presented as a strong assumption. Possessive constructions such as 'his car' have a potential presupposition (i.e. he has a car) which can be presented tentatively via expressions such as 'or something', as in [16].

[16] a. What's that guy doing in the parking lot?
b. He's looking for his car or something.

In [16b.], the speaker is not committed to the presupposition (he has a car) as an assumed fact. It is worth remembering that it is never the word or phrase that has a presupposition. Only speakers can have presuppositions.

Ordered entailments

Generally speaking, entailment is not a pragmatic concept (i.e. having to do with speaker meaning), but instead is considered a purely logical concept, symbolized by ⊩. Some examples of entailment for the sentence in [17] are presented in [18].

[17] Rover chased three squirrels. $(= p)$

[18] a. Something chased three squirrels. $(= q)$
     b. Rover did something to three squirrels. $(= r)$
     c. Rover chased three of something. $(= s)$
     d. Something happened. $(= t)$

In representing the relationship of entailment between [17] and [18a.] as $p \Vdash q$, we have simply symbolized a logical consequence. Let us say that in uttering the sentence in [17], the speaker is necessarily committed to the truth of a very large number of **background entailments** (only some of which are presented in [18 a.–d.]). On any occasion of utterance [17], however, the speaker will indicate how these entailments are to be ordered. That is, the speaker will communicate, typically by stress, which entailment is assumed to be in the foreground, or more important for interpreting intended meaning, than any others. For example, in uttering [19a.], the speaker indicates that the **foreground entailment**, and hence her main assumption, is that Rover chased a certain number of squirrels.

[19] a. Rover chased THREE squirrels.
     b. ROVER chased three squirrels.

In [19b.], the focus shifts to Rover, and the main assumption is that something chased three squirrels. One function of stress in English is, in this approach, clearly tied to marking the main assumption of the speaker in producing an utterance. As such, it allows the speaker to mark for the listener what the focus of the message is, and what is being assumed.

A very similar function is exhibited by a structure called an 'it-cleft' construction in English, as shown in [20].

[20] a. It was ROVER that chased the squirrels.
b. It wasn't ME who took your money.

In both examples in [20], the speaker can communicate what he or she believes the listener may already be thinking (i.e. the foreground entailment). In [20b.] that foreground entailment (someone took your money) is being made the shared knowledge in order for the denial of personal responsibility to be made. The utterance in [20b.] can be used to attribute the foreground entailment to the listener(s) without actually stating it (for example, as a possible accusation). It is one more example of more being communicated than is said.

5
Cooperation and implicature

In much of the preceding discussion, we have assumed that speakers and listeners involved in conversation are generally cooperating with each other. For example, for reference to be successful, it was proposed that collaboration was a necessary factor. In accepting speakers' presuppositions, listeners normally have to assume that a speaker who says 'my car' really does have the car that is mentioned and isn't trying to mislead the listener. This sense of cooperation is simply one in which people having a conversation are not normally assumed to be trying to confuse, trick, or withhold relevant information from each other. In most circumstances, this kind of cooperation is only the starting point for making sense of what is said.

In the middle of their lunch hour, one woman asks another how she likes the hamburger she is eating, and receives the answer in [1].

[1] A hamburger is a hamburger.

From a purely logical perspective, the reply in [1] seems to have no communicative value since it expresses something completely obvious. The example in [1] and other apparently pointless expressions like 'business is business' or 'boys will be boys', are called **tautologies**. If they are used in a conversation, clearly the speaker intends to communicate more than is said.

When the listener hears the expression in [1], she first has to assume that the speaker is being cooperative and intends to communicate something. That something must be more than just what the words mean. It is an additional conveyed meaning, called an **implicature**. By stating [1], the speaker expects that the listener will be able to work out, on the basis of what is already known, the implicature intended in this context.

Given the opportunity to evaluate the hamburger, the speaker of [1] has responded without an evaluation, thus one implicature is that she has no opinion, either good or bad, to express. Depending on other aspects of the context, additional implicatures (for example, the speaker thinks all hamburgers are the same) might be inferred.

Implicatures are primary examples of more being communicated than is said, but in order for them to be interpreted, some basic cooperative principle must first be assumed to be in operation.

The cooperative principle

Consider the following scenario. There is a woman sitting on a park bench and a large dog lying on the ground in front of the bench. A man comes along and sits down on the bench.

[2] Man: Does your dog bite?
Woman: No.
(The man reaches down to pet the dog. The dog bites the man's hand.)
Man: Ouch! Hey! You said your dog doesn't bite.
Woman: He doesn't. But that's not my dog.

One of the problems in this scenario has to do with communication. Specifically, it seems to be a problem caused by the man's assumption that more was communicated than was said. It isn't a problem with presupposition because the assumption in 'your dog' (i.e. the woman has a dog) is true for both speakers. The problem is the man's assumption that his question 'Does your dog bite?' and the woman's answer 'No' both apply to the dog in front of them. From the man's perspective, the woman's answer provides less information than expected. In other words, she might be expected to provide the information stated in the last line. Of course, if she had mentioned this information earlier, the story wouldn't be as funny. For the event to be funny, the woman has to give less information than is expected.

The concept of there being an expected amount of information provided in conversation is just one aspect of the more general idea that people involved in a conversation will cooperate with each other. (Of course, the woman in [2] may actually be indicating that she does not want to take part in any cooperative interaction with the stranger.) In most circumstances, the assumption of cooperation is so pervasive that it can be stated as a **cooperative principle** of conversation and elaborated in four sub principles, called **maxims**, as shown in Table 5.1.

The cooperative principle: Make your conversational contribution such as is required, at the stage at which it occurs, by the accepted purpose or direction of the talk exchange in which you are engaged.

The maxims

   Quantity
1. Make your contribution as informative as is required (for the current purposes of the exchange).
2. Do not make your contribution more informative than is required.

   Quality Try to make your contribution one that is true.
1. Do not say what you believe to be false.
2. Do not say that for which you lack adequate evidence.

   Relation Be relevant.

   Manner Be perspicuous.
1. Avoid obscurity of expression.
2. Avoid ambiguity.
3. Be brief (avoid unnecessary prolixity).
4. Be orderly.

TABLE 5.1 *The cooperative principle (following Grice 1975)*

It is important to recognize these maxims as unstated assumptions we have in conversations. We assume that people are normally going to provide an appropriate amount of information (unlike the woman in [2]); we assume that they are telling the truth, being relevant, and trying to be as clear as they can. Because these principles are assumed in normal interaction, speakers rarely mention them. However, there are certain kinds of expressions speakers use to mark that they may be in danger of *not* fully adhering to the principles. These kinds of expressions are called hedges.

Hedges

The importance of the maxim of **quality** for cooperative interaction in English may be best measured by the number of expressions we use to indicate that what we're saying may not be totally accurate. The initial phrases in [3a.–c.] and the final phrase in [3d.] are notes to the listener regarding the accuracy of the main statement.

[3] a. As far as I know, they're married.
    b. I may be mistaken, but I thought I saw a wedding ring on her finger.
    c. I'm not sure if this is right, but I heard it was a secret ceremony in Hawaii.
    d. He couldn't live without her, I guess.

The conversational context for the examples in [3] might be a recent rumor involving a couple known to the speakers. Cautious notes, or **hedges**, of this type can also be used to show that the speaker is conscious of the **quantity** maxim, as in the initial phrases in [4a.–c.], produced in the course of a speaker's account of her recent vacation.

[4] a. As you probably know, I am terrified of bugs.
    b. So, to cut a long story short, we grabbed our stuff and ran.
    c. I won't bore you with all the details, but it was an exciting trip.

Markers tied to the expectation of relevance (from the maxim of **relation**) can be found in the middle of speakers' talk when they say things like 'Oh, by the way' and go on to mention some potentially unconnected information during a conversation. Speakers also seem to use expressions like 'anyway', or 'well, anyway', to indicate that they may have drifted into a discussion of some possibly non-relevant material and want to stop. Some expressions which may act as hedges on the expectation of relevance are shown as the initial phrases in [5a.–c.], from an office meeting.

[5] a. I don't know if this is important, but some of the files are missing.

b. This may sound like a dumb question, but whose hand writing is this?

c. Not to change the subject, but is this related to the budget?

The awareness of the expectations of **manner** may also lead speakers to produce hedges of the type shown in the initial phrases in [6a.–c.], heard during an account of a crash.

[6] a. This may be a bit confused, but I remember being in a car.

b. I'm not sure if this makes sense, but the car had no lights.

c. I don't know if this is clear at all, but I think the other car was reversing.

All of these examples of hedges are good indications that the speakers are not only aware of the maxims, but that they want to show that they are trying to observe them. Perhaps such forms also communicate the speakers' concern that their listeners judge them to be cooperative conversational partners.

There are, however, some circumstances where speakers may not follow the expectations of the cooperative principle. In court-rooms and classrooms, witnesses and students are often called upon to tell people things which are already well-known to those people (thereby violating the quantity maxim). Such specialized institutional talk is clearly different from conversation.

However, even in conversation, a speaker may 'opt out' of the maxim expectations by using expressions like 'No comment' or 'My lips are sealed' in response to a question. An interesting aspect of such expressions is that, although they are typically not 'as informative as is required' in the context, they are naturally inter-preted as communicating more than is said (i.e. the speaker knows the answer). This typical reaction (i.e. there must be something 'special' here) of listeners to any apparent violation of the maxims is actually the key to the notion of conversational implicature.

Conversational implicature

The basic assumption in conversation is that, unless otherwise indicated, the participants are adhering to the cooperative principle and the maxims. In example [7], Dexter may appear to be violating the requirements of the quantity maxim.

[7] Charlene: I hope you brought the bread and the cheese.
Dexter: Ah, I brought the bread.

After hearing Dexter's response in [7], Charlene has to assume that Dexter is cooperating and not totally unaware of the quantity maxim. But he didn't mention the cheese. If he had brought the cheese, he would say so, because he would be adhering to the quantity maxim. He must intend that she infer that what is not mentioned was not brought. In this case, Dexter has conveyed more than he said via a **conversational implicature.**

We can represent the structure of what was said, with b (= bread) and c (= cheese) as in [8]. Using the symbol +> for an implicature, we can also represent the additional conveyed meaning.

[8] Charlene: b & c?
Dexter: b (+> NOT c)

It is important to note that it is speakers who communicate meaning via implicatures and it is listeners who recognize those communicated meanings via inference. The inferences selected are those which will preserve the assumption of cooperation.

Generalized conversational implicatures

In the case of example [7], particularly as represented in [8], no special background knowledge of the context of utterance is required in order to make the necessary inferences. The same process of calculating the implicature will take place if Doobie asks Mary about inviting her friends Bella (= b) and Cathy (= c) to a party, as in [9a.], and gets the reply in [9b.]. The context is different from [7], but the general process of identifying the implicature is the same as in [8].

[9] a. Doobie: Did you invite Bella and Cathy? (b & c?)
     b. Mary: I invited Bella.   (b +> NOT c)

When no special knowledge is required in the context to calculate the additional conveyed meaning, as in [7] to [9], it is called a **generalized conversational implicature**. One common example in English involves any phrase with an indefinite article of the type 'a/an X', such as 'a garden' and 'a child' as in [10]. These phrases are typically interpreted according to the generalized conversational implicature that: an X +> not speaker's X.

> [10] I was sitting in a garden one day. A child looked over the
>   fence.

The implicatures in [10], that the garden and the child mentioned are not the speaker's, are calculated on the principle that if the speaker was capable of being more specific (i.e. more informative, following the quantity maxim), then he or she would have said 'my garden' and 'my child'.

A number of other generalized conversational implicatures are commonly communicated on the basis of a scale of values and are consequently known as scalar implicatures.

Scalar implicatures

Certain information is always communicated by choosing a word which expresses one value from a scale of values. This is particularly obvious in terms for expressing quantity, as shown in the scales in [11], where terms are listed from the highest to the lowest value.

> [11] < all, most, many, some, few>
>   < always, often, sometimes>

When producing an utterance, a speaker selects the word from the scale which is the most informative and truthful (quantity and quality) in the circumstances, as in [12].

> [12] I'm studying linguistics and I've completed some of the
>   required courses.

By choosing 'some' in [12], the speaker creates an implicature (+> not all). This is one scalar implicature of uttering [12]. The basis of **scalar implicature** is that, when any form in a scale is asserted, the negative of all forms higher on the scale is implicated. The first scale in [11] had 'all', 'most', and 'many', higher than 'some'. Given the definition of scalar implicature, it should follow that, in saying 'some of the required courses', the speaker also creates other implicatures (for example, +> not most, +> not many).

If the speaker goes on to describe those linguistics courses as in [13], then we can identify some more scalar implicatures.

[13] They're sometimes really interesting.

By using 'sometimes' in [13], the speaker communicates, via implicature, the negative of forms higher on the scale of frequency (+> not always, +> not often).

There are many scalar implicatures produced by the use of expressions that we may not immediately consider to be part of any scale. For example, the utterance of [14a.] will be interpreted as implicating '+> not certain' as a higher value on the scale of 'likelihood' and [14b.] '+> not must' on a scale of 'obligation' and '+> not frozen' on a scale of 'coldness'.

[14] a. It's possible that they were delayed.
      b. This should be stored in a cool place.

One noticeable feature of scalar implicatures is that when speakers correct themselves on some detail, as in [15], they typically cancel one of the scalar implicatures.

[15] I got some of this jewelry in Hong Kong—um actually I think I got most of it there.

In [15], the speaker initially implicates '+> not most' by saying 'some', but then corrects herself by actually asserting 'most'. That final assertion is still likely to be interpreted, however, with a scalar implicature (+> not all).

Particularized conversational implicatures

In the preceding examples, the implicatures have been calculated without special knowledge of any particular context. However, most of the time, our conversations take place in very specific contexts in which locally recognized inferences are assumed. Such inferences are required to work out the conveyed meanings which result from **particularized conversational implicatures**. As an illustration, consider example [16], where Tom's response does not appear on the surface to adhere to relevance. (A simply relevant answer would be 'Yes' or 'No'.)

[16] Rick: Hey, coming to the wild party tonight?
Tom: My parents are visiting.

In order to make Tom's response relevant, Rick has to draw on some assumed knowledge that one college student in this setting expects another to have. Tom will be spending that evening with his parents, and time spent with parents is quiet (consequently +> Tom not at party).

Because they are by far the most common, particularized conversational implicatures are typically just called implicatures. A further example, in which the speaker appears not to adhere to (i.e. to 'flout') the maxim of manner, is presented in [17].

[17] Ann: Where are you going with the dog?
Sam: To the V-E-T.

In the local context of these speakers, the dog is known to recognize the word 'vet', and to hate being taken there, so Sam produces a more elaborate, spelled out (i.e. less brief) version of his message, implicating that he doesn't want the dog to know the answer to the question just asked.

In [18], Leila has just walked into Mary's office and noticed all the work on her desk. Mary's response seems to flout the maxim of relevance.

[18] Leila: Whoa! Has your boss gone crazy?
Mary: Let's go get some coffee.

In order to preserve the assumption of cooperation, Leila will have to infer some local reason (for example, the boss may be nearby) why Mary makes an apparently non-relevant remark. The implicature here is essentially that Mary cannot answer the question in that context.

In addition to these fairly prosaic examples of implicatures, there are other more entertaining examples, as in [19] and [20], where the responses initially appear to flout relevance.

[19] Bert: Do you like ice-cream?
Ernie: Is the Pope Catholic?

[20] Bert: Do vegetarians eat hamburgers?
Ernie: Do chickens have lips?

In [19], Ernie's response does not provide a 'yes' or 'no' answer. Bert must assume that Ernie is being cooperative, so he considers Ernie's 'Pope' question and clearly the answer is 'Yes'. So, the answer is known, but the nature of Ernie's response also implicates that the answer to the question was 'Obviously, yes!'. An additional conveyed meaning in such a case is that, because the answer was so obvious, the question did not need to be asked. Example [20] provides the same type of inferencing with an answer 'Of course not!' as part of the implicature.

Properties of conversational implicatures

So far, all the implicatures we have considered have been situated within conversation, with the inferences being made by people who hear the utterances and attempt to maintain the assumption of cooperative interaction. Because these implicatures are part of what is communicated and not said, speakers can always deny that they intended to communicate such meanings. Conversational implicatures are deniable. They can be explicitly denied (or alternatively, reinforced) in different ways. To take a simple example, there is a standard implicature associated with stating a number, that the speaker means *only* that number, as shown in [21].

[21] You have won five dollars! (+> ONLY five)

As shown in [22], however, it is quite easy for a speaker to suspend the implicature (+> only) using the expression 'at least' [22a.], or to cancel the implicature by adding further information, often following the expression 'in fact' [22b.], or to reinforce the implicature with additional information, as in [22c.].

[22] a. You've won at least five dollars!
b. You've won five dollars, in fact, you've won ten!
c. You've won five dollars, that's four more than one!

We have already noted with many of the previous examples that implicatures can be calculated by the listeners via inference. In terms of their defining properties, then, conversational implicatures can be calculated, suspended, cancelled, and reinforced. None of these properties apply to conventional implicatures.

Conventional implicatures

In contrast to all the conversational implicatures discussed so far, **conventional implicatures** are not based on the cooperative principle or the maxims. They don't have to occur in conversation, and they don't depend on special contexts for their interpretation. Not unlike lexical presuppositions, conventional implicatures are associated with specific words and result in additional conveyed meanings when those words are used. The English conjunction 'but' is one of these words. The interpretation of any utterance of the type p *but* q will be based on the conjunction p & q plus an implicature of 'contrast' between the information in p and the information in q. In [23], the fact that 'Mary suggested black' (= p) is contrasted, via the conventional implicature of 'but', with my choosing white (= q).

[23] a. Mary suggested black, but I chose white.
 b. p & q (+> p is in contrast to q)

Other English words such as 'even' and 'yet' also have conventional implicatures. When 'even' is included in any sentence describing an event, there is an implicature of 'contrary to expectation'. Thus, in [24] there are two events reported (i.e. John's coming and John's helping) with the conventional implicature of 'even' adding a 'contrary to expectation' interpretation of those events.

[24] a. Even John came to the party.
 b. He even helped tidy up afterwards.

The conventional implicature of 'yet' is that the present situation is expected to be different, or perhaps the opposite, at a later time. In uttering the statement in [25a.], the speaker produces an implicature that she expects the statement 'Dennis is here' (= p) to be true later, as indicated in [25b.].

[25] a. Dennis isn't here yet.   (= NOT p)
 b. NOT p is true   (+> p expected to be true later)

It may be possible to treat the so-called different 'meanings' of 'and' in English (discussed in Chapter 1) as instances of conventional implicature in different structures. When two statements containing static information are joined by 'and', as in [26a.], the implicature is simply 'in addition' or 'plus'. When the two statements contain dynamic, action-related information, as in [26b.], the implicature of 'and' is 'and then' indicating sequence.

[26] a. Yesterday, Mary was happy
and ready to work. $(p \ \& \ q, +> p \ plus \ q)$
b. She put on her clothes and left
the house. $(p \ \& \ q, +> q \ after \ p)$

Because of the different implicatures, the two parts of [26a.] can be reversed with little difference in meaning, but there is a big change in meaning if the two parts of [26b.] are reversed.

For many linguists, the notion of 'implicature' is one of the central concepts in pragmatics. An implicature is certainly a prime example of more being communicated than is said. For those same linguists, another central concept in pragmatics is the observation that utterances perform actions, generally known as 'speech acts'.

6
Speech acts and events

In attempting to express themselves, people do not only produce utterances containing grammatical structures and words, they perform actions via those utterances. If you work in a situation where a boss has a great deal of power, then the boss's utterance of the expression in [1] is more than just a statement.

[1] You're fired.

The utterance in [1] can be used to perform the act of ending your employment. However, the actions performed by utterances do not have to be as dramatic or as unpleasant as in [1]. The action can be quite pleasant, as in the compliment performed by [2a.], the acknowledgement of thanks in [2b.], or the expression of surprise in [2c.].

[2] a. You're so delicious.
    b. You're welcome.
    c. You're crazy!

Actions performed via utterances are generally called **speech acts** and, in English, are commonly given more specific labels, such as apology, complaint, compliment, invitation, promise, or request.

These descriptive terms for different kinds of speech acts apply to the speaker's communicative intention in producing an utterance. The speaker normally expects that his or her communicative intention will be recognized by the hearer. Both speaker and hearer are usually helped in this process by the circumstances surrounding the utterance. These circumstances, including other utterances, are called the **speech event**. In many ways, it is the nature of the speech event that determines the interpretation of an utterance as performing a particular speech act. On a wintry day, the speaker reaches for a cup of tea, believing that it has been freshly made, takes a sip, and produces the utterance in [3]. It is likely to be interpreted as a complaint.

[3] This tea is really cold!

Changing the circumstances to a really hot summer's day with the speaker being given a glass of iced tea by the hearer, taking a sip and producing the utterance in [3], it is likely to be interpreted as praise. If the same utterance can be interpreted as two different kinds of speech act, then obviously no simple one utterance to one action correspondence will be possible. It also means that there is more to the interpretation of a speech act than can be found in the utterance alone.

Speech acts

On any occasion, the action performed by producing an utterance will consist of three related acts. There is first a **locutionary act**, which is the basic act of utterance, or producing a meaningful linguistic expression. If you have difficulty with actually forming the sounds and words to create a meaningful utterance in a language (for example, because it's foreign or you're tongue-tied), then you might fail to produce a locutionary act. Producing 'Aha mokofa' in English will not normally count as a locutionary act, whereas [4] will.

[4] I've just made some coffee.

Mostly we don't just produce well-formed utterances with no purpose. We form an utterance with some kind of function in mind. This is the second dimension, or the **illocutionary act**. The illocutionary act is performed via the communicative force of an utterance. We might utter [4] to make a statement, an offer, an explanation, or for some other communicative purpose. This is also generally known as the **illocutionary force** of the utterance.

We do not, of course, simply create an utterance with a function without intending it to have an effect. This is the third dimension, the **perlocutionary act**. Depending on the circumstances, you will utter [4] on the assumption that the hearer will recognize the effect you intended (for example, to account for a wonderful smell, or to get the hearer to drink some coffee). This is also generally known as the **perlocutionary effect.**

Of these three dimensions, the most discussed is illocutionary force. Indeed, the term 'speech act' is generally interpreted quite narrowly to mean only the illocutionary force of an utterance. The illocutionary force of an utterance is what it 'counts as'. The same locutionary act, as shown in [5a.], can count as a prediction [5b.], a promise [5c.], or a warning [5d.]. These different analyses [5b.–d.] of the utterance in [5a.] represent different illocutionary forces.

[5] a. I'll see you later. (= A)
    b. [I predict that] A.
    c. [I promise you that] A.
    d. [I warn you that] A.

One problem with the examples in [5] is that the same utterance can potentially have quite different illocutionary forces (for example, promise versus warning). How can speakers assume that the intended illocutionary force will be recognized by the hearer? That question has been addressed by considering two things: Illocutionary Force Indicating Devices and felicity conditions.

IFIDs

The most obvious device for indicating the illocutionary force (the **Illocutionary Force Indicating Device**, or **IFID**) is an expression of the type shown in [6] where there is a slot for a verb that explicitly names the illocutionary act being performed. Such a verb can be called a **performative verb** (Vp).

[6] I (Vp) you that …

In the preceding examples, [5c.,d.], 'promise' and 'warn' would be the performative verbs and, if stated, would be very clear IFIDs. Speakers do not always 'perform' their speech acts so explicitly, but they sometimes describe the speech act being performed. Imagine the telephone conversation in [7], between a man trying to contact Mary, and Mary's friend.

[7] Him: Can I talk to Mary?
Her: No, she's not here.
Him: I'm asking you—can I talk to her?
Her: And I'm telling you—SHE'S NOT HERE!

In this scenario, each speaker has described, and drawn attention to, the illocutionary force ('ask' and 'tell') of their utterances.

Most of the time, however, there is no performative verb mentioned. Other IFIDs which can be identified are word order, stress, and intonation, as shown in the different versions of the same basic elements (Y–G) in [8].

[8] a. You're going!   [I tell you Y–G]
b. You're going?   [I request confirmation about Y–G]
c. Are you going?   [I ask you if Y–G]

While other devices, such as a lowered voice quality for a warning or a threat, might be used to indicate illocutionary force, the utterance also has to be produced under certain conventional conditions to count as having the intended illocutionary force.

Felicity conditions

There are certain expected or appropriate circumstances, technically known as **felicity conditions**, for the performance of a speech act to be recognized as intended. For some clear cases, such as [9], the performance will be infelicitous (inappropriate) if the speaker is not a specific person in a special context (in this case, a judge in a courtroom).

[9] I sentence you to six months in prison.

In everyday contexts among ordinary people, there are also preconditions on speech acts. There are **general conditions** on the participants, for example, that they can understand the language being used and that they are not play-acting or being nonsensical. Then there are **content conditions**. For example, for both a promise and a warning, the content of the utterance must be about a future event. A further content condition for a promise requires that the future event will be a future act of the speaker.

The **preparatory conditions** for a promise are significantly different from those for a warning. When I promise to do something, there are two preparatory conditions: first, the event will not happen by itself, and second, the event will have a beneficial effect. When I utter a warning, there are the following preparatory conditions: it isn't clear that the hearer knows the event will occur, the speaker does think the event will occur, and the event will not have a beneficial effect. Related to these conditions is the **sincerity condition** that, for a promise, the speaker genuinely intends to carry out the future action, and, for a warning, the speaker genuinely believes that the future event will not have a beneficial effect.

Finally, there is the **essential condition**, which covers the fact that by the act of uttering a promise, I thereby intend to create an obligation to carry out the action as promised. In other words, the utterance changes my state from non-obligation to obligation. Similarly, with a warning, under the essential condition, the utterance changes my state from non-informing of a bad future event to informing. This essential condition thus combines with a specification of what must be in the utterance content, the context, and the speaker's intentions, in order for a specific speech act to be appropriately (felicitously) performed.

The performative hypothesis

One way to think about the speech acts being performed via utterances is to assume that underlying every utterance (U) there is a clause, similar to [6] presented earlier, containing a performative verb (Vp) which makes the illocutionary force explicit. This is known as the **performative hypothesis** and the basic format of the underlying clause is shown in [10].

[10] I (hereby) Vp you (that) U

In this clause, the subject must be first person singular ('I'), followed by the adverb 'hereby', indicating that the utterance 'counts as' an action by being uttered. There is also a performative verb (Vp) in the present tense and an indirect object in second person singular ('you'). This underlying clause will always make explicit, as in [11b.] and [12b.], what, in utterances such as [11a.] and [12a.], is implicit.

[11] a. Clean up this mess!
      b. I hereby order you that you clean up this mess.

[12] a. The work was done by Elaine and myself.
      b. I hereby tell you that the work was done by Elaine and
         myself.

Examples like [11b.] and [12b.] (normally without 'hereby'), are used by speakers as **explicit performatives**. Examples like [11a.] and [12a.] are **implicit performatives**, sometimes called **primary performatives**.

The advantage of this type of analysis is that it makes clear just what elements are involved in the production and interpretation of utterances. In syntax, a reflexive pronoun (like 'myself' in [12]) requires the occurrence of an antecedent (in this case 'I') within the same sentence structure. The explicit performative in [12b.] provides the 'I' element. Similarly, when you say to someone, 'Do it yourself!', the reflexive in 'yourself' is made possible by the antecedent 'you' in the explicit version ('I order you that you do it yourself'). Another advantage is to show that some adverbs such as 'honestly', or adverbial clauses such as 'because I may be late', as shown in [13], naturally attach to the explicit performative clause rather than the implicit version.

[13] a. Honestly, he's a scoundrel.
      b. What time is it, because I may be late?

In [13a.], it is the telling part (the performative verb) that is being done 'honestly' and, in [13b.], it is the act of asking (the performative again) that is being justified by the 'because I may be late' clause.

There are some technical disadvantages to the performative hypothesis. For example, uttering the explicit performative version of a command [11b.] has a much more serious impact than uttering the implicit version [11a.]. The two versions are consequently not equivalent. It is also difficult to know exactly what the performative verb (or verbs) might be for some utterances. Although the speaker and hearer might recognize the utterance in [14a.] as an insult, it would be very strange to have [14b.] as an explicit version.

[14] a. You're dumber than a rock.
      b. ? I hereby insult you that you're dumber than a rock.

The really practical problem with any analysis based on identifying explicit performatives is that, in principle, we simply do not know how many performative verbs there are in any language. Instead of trying to list all the possible explicit performatives, and then distinguish among all of them, some more general classifications of types of speech acts are usually used.

Speech act classification

One general classification system lists five types of general functions performed by speech acts: declarations, representatives, expressives, directives, and commissives.

Declarations are those kinds of speech acts that change the world via their utterance. As the examples in [15] illustrate, the speaker has to have a special institutional role, in a specific context, in order to perform a declaration appropriately.

[15] a. Priest: I now pronounce you husband and wife.
b. Referee: You're out!
c. Jury Foreman: We find the defendant guilty.

In using a declaration, the speaker changes the world via words.

Representatives are those kinds of speech acts that state what the speaker believes to be the case or not. Statements of fact, assertions, conclusions, and descriptions, as illustrated in [16], are all examples of the speaker representing the world as he or she believes it is.

[16] a. The earth is flat.
b. Chomsky didn't write about peanuts.
c. It was a warm sunny day.

In using a representative, the speaker makes words fit the world (of belief).

Expressives are those kinds of speech acts that state what the speaker feels. They express psychological states and can be statements of pleasure, pain, likes, dislikes, joy, or sorrow. As illustrated in [17], they can be caused by something the speaker does or the hearer does, but they are about the speaker's experience.

[17] a. I'm really sorry!
b. Congratulations!
c. Oh, yes, great, mmmm, ssahh!

In using an expressive, the speaker makes words fit the world (of feeling).

Directives are those kinds of speech acts that speakers use to get someone else to do something. They express what the speaker wants. They are commands, orders, requests, suggestions, and, as illustrated in [18], they can be positive or negative.

[18] a. Gimme a cup of coffee. Make it black.
    b. Could you lend me a pen, please?
    c. Don't touch that.

In using a directive, the speaker attempts to make the world fit the words (via the hearer).

Commissives are those kinds of speech acts that speakers use to commit themselves to some future action. They express what the speaker intends. They are promises, threats, refusals, pledges, and, as shown in [19], they can be performed by the speaker alone, or by the speaker as a member of a group.

[19] a. I'll be back.
    b. I'm going to get it right next time.
    c. We will not do that.

In using a commissive, the speaker undertakes to make the world fit the words (via the speaker).

These five general functions of speech acts, with their key features, are summarized in Table 6.1.

Direct and indirect speech acts

A different approach to distinguishing types of speech acts can be made on the basis of structure. A fairly simple structural distinction between three general types of speech acts is provided, in English, by the three basic sentence types. As shown in [20], there is an easily recognized relationship between the three structural forms (declarative, interrogative, imperative) and the three general communicative functions (statement, question, command/request).

[20] a. You wear a seat belt.   (declarative)
    b. Do you wear a seat belt?   (interrogative)
    c. Wear a seat belt!   (imperative)

Whenever there is a direct relationship between a structure and a

Speech act type	Direction of fit	S = speaker; X = situation
Declarations	words change the world	S causes X
Representatives	make words fit the world	S believes X
Expressives	make words fit the world	S feels X
Directives	make the world fit words	S wants X
Commissives	make the world fit words	S intends X

TABLE 6.1 *The five general functions of speech acts (following Searle 1979)*

function, we have a **direct speech act**. Whenever there is an indirect relationship between a structure and a function, we have an **indirect speech act**. Thus, a declarative used to make a statement is a direct speech act, but a declarative used to make a request is an indirect speech act. As illustrated in [21], the utterance in [21a.] is a declarative. When it is used to make a statement, as paraphrased in [21b.], it is functioning as a direct speech act. When it is used to make a command/request, as paraphrased in [21c.], it is functioning as an indirect speech act.

[21] a. It's cold outside.
b. I hereby tell you about the weather.
c. I hereby request of you that you close the door.

Different structures can be used to accomplish the same basic function, as in [22], where the speaker wants the addressee not to stand in front of the TV. The basic function of all the utterances in [22] is a command/request, but only the imperative structure in [22a.] represents a direct speech act. The interrogative structure in [22b.] is not being used only as a question, hence it is an indirect speech act. The declarative structures in [22c.] and [22d.] are also indirect requests.

[22] a. Move out of the way!
b. Do you have to stand in front of the TV?
c. You're standing in front of the TV.
d. You'd make a better door than a window.

One of the most common types of indirect speech act in English, as shown in [23], has the form of an interrogative, but is not typically used to ask a question (i.e. we don't expect only an answer, we expect action). The examples in [23] are normally understood as requests.

[23] a. Could you pass the salt?
b. Would you open this?

Indeed, there is a typical pattern in English whereby asking a question about the hearer's assumed ability ('Can you?', 'Could you?') or future likelihood with regard to doing something ('Will you?', 'Would you?') normally counts as a request to actually do that something.

Indirect speech acts are generally associated with greater politeness in English than direct speech acts. In order to understand why, we have to look at a bigger picture than just a single utterance performing a single speech act.

Speech events

We can treat an indirect request (for example, the utterances in [23]) as being a matter of asking whether the necessary conditions for a request are in place. For example, a preparatory condition is that the speaker assumes the hearer is able to, or CAN, perform the action. A content condition concerns future action, that the hearer WILL perform the action. This pattern is illustrated in [24].

[24] Indirect requests

a. Content condition	Future act of hearer (= hearer WILL do X)	'WILL you do X?'
b. Preparatory condition	Hearer is able to perform act (= hearer CAN do X)	'CAN you do X?'

c. Questioning a hearer-based condition for making a request results in an indirect request.

There is a definite difference between asking someone to do X and asking someone if the preconditions for doing X are in place, as in

[24c]. Asking about preconditions technically doesn't count as making a request, but does allow the hearer to react 'as if' the request had been made. Because a request is an imposition by the speaker on the hearer, it is better, in most social circumstances, for the speaker to avoid a direct imposition via a direct request. When the speaker asks about preconditions, no direct request is made.

The preceding discussion is essentially about one person trying to get another person to do something without risking refusal or causing offense. However, this type of situation does not consist of a single utterance. It is a social situation involving participants who necessarily have a social relationship of some kind, and who, on a specific occasion, may have particular goals.

We can look at the set of utterances produced in this kind of situation as a **speech event**. A speech event is an activity in which participants interact via language in some conventional way to arrive at some outcome. It may include an obvious central speech act, such as 'I don't really like this', as in a speech event of 'complaining', but it will also include other utterances leading up to and subsequently reacting to that central action. In most cases, a 'request' is not made by means of a single speech act suddenly uttered. Requesting is typically a speech event, as illustrated in [25].

[25] Him: Oh, Mary, I'm glad you're here.
Her: What's up?
Him: I can't get my computer to work.
Her: Is it broken?
Him: I don't think so.
Her: What's it doing?
Him: I don't know. I'm useless with computers.
Her: What kind is it?
Him: It's a Mac. Do you use them?
Her: Yeah.
Him: Do you have a minute?
Her: Sure.
Him: Oh, great.

The extended interaction in [25] may be called a 'requesting' speech event without a central speech act of request. Notice that there is no actual request from 'him' to 'her' to do anything. We might characterize the question 'Do you have a minute?' as a 'pre-request', allowing the receiver to say that she's busy or that she has to be somewhere else. In this context, the response 'Sure' is taken to be an acknowledgement not only of having time available, but a willingness to perform the unstated action. The analysis of speech events is clearly another way of studying how more gets communicated than is said.

The usefulness of speech act analysis is in illustrating the kinds of things we can do with words and identifying some of the conventional utterance forms we use to perform specific actions. However, we do need to look at more extended interaction to understand how those actions are carried out and interpreted within speech events.

7
Politeness and interaction

In much of the preceding discussion, the small-scale scenarios presented to illustrate language in use have been populated by people with virtually no social lives. Yet, much of what we say, and a great deal of what we communicate, is determined by our social relationships. A linguistic interaction is necessarily a social interaction.

In order to make sense of what is said in an interaction, we have to look at various factors which relate to social distance and closeness. Some of these factors are established prior to an interaction and hence are largely external factors. They typically involve the relative status of the participants, based on social values tied to such things as age and power. For example, speakers who see themselves as lower status in English-speaking contexts tend to mark social distance between themselves and higher status speakers by using address forms that include a title and a last name, but not the first name (for example, Mrs Clinton, Mr Adams, Dr Dang). We take part in a wide range of interactions (mostly with strangers) where the social distance determined by external factors is dominant.

However, there are other factors, such as amount of imposition or degree of friendliness, which are often negotiated during an interaction. These are internal to the interaction and can result in the initial social distance changing and being marked as less, or more, during its course. This may result, for example, in participants moving from a title-plus-last name to a first-name basis within the talk. These internal factors are typically more relevant to participants whose social relationships are actually in the process of being worked out within the interaction.

Both types of factors, external and internal, have an influence not only on what we say, but also on how we are interpreted. In many cases, the interpretation goes beyond what we might have intended to convey and includes evaluations such as 'rude' and 'inconsiderate', or 'considerate' and 'thoughtful'. Recognizing the impact of such evaluations makes it very clear that more is being communicated than is said. The investigation of that impact is normally carried out in terms of politeness.

Politeness

It is possible to treat politeness as a fixed concept, as in the idea of 'polite social behavior', or etiquette, within a culture. It is also possible to specify a number of different general principles for being polite in social interaction within a particular culture. Some of these might include being tactful, generous, modest, and sympathetic toward others. Let us assume that participants in an interaction are generally aware that such norms and principles exist in the society at large. Within an interaction, however, there is a more narrowly specified type of politeness at work. In order to describe it, we need the concept of face.

As a technical term, **face** means the public self-image of a person. It refers to that emotional and social sense of self that everyone has and expects everyone else to recognize. **Politeness**, in an interaction, can then be defined as the means employed to show awareness of another person's face. In this sense, politeness can be accomplished in situations of social distance or closeness. Showing awareness for another person's face when that other seems socially distant is often described in terms of respect or deference. Showing the equivalent awareness when the other is socially close is often described in terms of friendliness, camaraderie, or solidarity. The first type might be found in a student's question to his teacher, shown as [1a.], and a second type in the friend's question to the same individual, as in [1b.].

[1] a. Excuse me, Mr Buckingham, but can I talk to you for a minute?
     b. Hey, Bucky, got a minute?

It follows from this type of approach that there will be different kinds of politeness associated (and marked linguistically) with the assumption of relative social distance or closeness. In most English-speaking contexts, the participants in an interaction often have to determine, as they speak, the relative social distance between them, and hence their 'face wants'.

Face wants

In this discussion, let's assume that the participants involved in interactions are not living in a context which has created rigidly fixed social relationships. Within their everyday social interactions, people generally behave as if their expectations concerning their public self-image, or their **face wants**, will be respected. If a speaker says something that represents a threat to another individual's expectations regarding self-image, it is described as a **face threatening act**. Alternatively, given the possibility that some action might be interpreted as a threat to another's face, the speaker can say something to lessen the possible threat. This is called a **face saving act**.

Imagine a late night scene, where a young neighbor is playing his music very loud and an older couple are trying to sleep. One of them, in [2], proposes a face threatening act and the other suggests a face saving act.

[2] Him: I'm going to tell him to stop that awful noise right now!

Her: Perhaps you could just ask him if he is going to stop soon because it's getting a bit late and people need to get to sleep.

Because it is generally expected that each person will attempt to respect the face wants of others, there are many different ways of performing face saving acts.

Negative and positive face

When we attempt to save another's face, we can pay attention to their negative face wants or their positive face wants. A person's **negative face** is the need to be independent, to have freedom of action, and not to be imposed on by others. The word 'negative' here doesn't mean 'bad', it's just the opposite pole from 'positive'. A person's **positive face** is the need to be accepted, even liked, by others, to be treated as a member of the same group, and to know that his or her wants are shared by others. In simple terms, negative face is the need to be independent and positive face is the need to be connected.

So, a face saving act which is oriented to the person's negative face will tend to show deference, emphasize the importance of the other's time or concerns, and even include an apology for the imposition or interruption. This is also called **negative politeness**. A face saving act which is concerned with the person's positive face will tend to show solidarity, emphasize that both speakers want the same thing, and that they have a common goal. This is also called **positive politeness**.

Self and other: say nothing

One way to see the relevance of the relationship between these politeness concepts and language use is to take a single speech event and map out the different interpretations associated with different possible expressions used within that event. For example, you arrive at an important lecture, pull out your notebook to take notes, but discover that you don't have anything to write with. You think that the person sitting next to you may provide the solution. In this scenario, you are going to be 'Self', and the person next to you is going to be 'Other'.

Your first choice is whether to say something or not. You can, of course, rummage in your bag, search rather obviously through your pockets, go back into your bag, without uttering a word, but with the vague intention that your problem will be recognized. This 'say nothing' approach may or may not work, but if it does, it's because the other offers and not because the self asks, as in [3].

[3] Self: (looks in bag)
    Other: (offers pen) Here, use this.

Many people seem to prefer to have their needs recognized by others without having to express those needs in language. When those needs are recognized, as in [3], then clearly more has been communicated than was said.

Say something: off and on record

Even if you decide to say something, you don't actually have to ask for anything. You can (perhaps after your search through your bag) simply produce a statement of the type in [4a.] or [4b.].

[4] a. Uh, I forgot my pen.
 b. Hmm, I wonder where I put my pen.

These, and other similar types of statement, are not directly addressed to the other. The other can act as if the statements have not even been heard. They are technically described as being **off record**. In casual descriptions, they might be referred to as 'hints'. Once again, an off record statement may or may not succeed (as a means of getting a pen), but if it does, it will be because more has been communicated than was said.

In contrast to such off record statements, you can directly address the other as a means of expressing your needs. These direct address forms are technically described as being **on record**. The most direct approach, using imperative forms such as those in [5], is known as **bald on record**. The other person is directly asked for something.

[5] a. Give me a pen.
 b. Lend me your pen.

These bald on record forms may be followed by expressions like 'please' and 'would you?' which serve to soften the demand and are called **mitigating devices**.

It is tempting to equate the bald on record approach with all direct command forms (i.e. imperatives). This would be misleading because imperative forms are often used by close familiars without being interpreted as commands. Examples would be a friend of-fering something to eat, as in [6a.], or trying to help you, as in [6b.].

[6] a. Have some more cake.
 b. Gimme that wet umbrella.

Emergency situations also occasion the use of direct commands, regardless of who is being addressed, as when danger prompts use of the expressions in [7].

[7] a. Don't touch that!
 b. Get out of here!

There are, consequently, some social circumstances where using a direct command as a bald on record expression is considered appropriate among social equals.

However, generally speaking, bald on record expressions are associated with speech events where the speaker assumes that he or she has power over the other (for example, in military contexts) and can control the other's behavior with words. In everyday interaction between social equals, such bald on record behavior would potentially represent a threat to the other's face and would generally be avoided. Avoiding a face threatening act is accomplished by face saving acts which use positive or negative politeness strategies.

Positive and negative politeness

A **positive politeness strategy** leads the requester to appeal to a common goal, and even friendship, via expressions such as those in [8].

[8] a. How about letting me use your pen?
    b. Hey, buddy, I'd appreciate it if you'd let me use your pen.

These on record expressions do represent a greater risk for the speaker of suffering a refusal and may be preceded by some 'getting to know you' talk, of the kind presented in [9], designed to establish the necessary common ground for this strategy.

[9] Hi. How's it going? Okay if I sit here? We must be interested in the same crazy stuff. You take a lot of notes too, huh? Say, do me a big favor and let me use one of your pens.

However, in most English-speaking contexts, a face saving act is more commonly performed via a **negative politeness strategy**. The most typical form used is a question containing a modal verb such as [10a.].

[10] a. Could you lend me a pen?
     b. I'm sorry to bother you, but can I ask you for a pen or something?
     c. I know you're busy, but might I ask you if—em—if you

happen to have an extra pen that I could, you know—eh—maybe borrow?

Using this strategy also results in forms which contain expressions of apology for the imposition, of the type shown in [10b.]. More elaborate negative politeness work can sometimes be heard in extended talk, often with hesitations, similar to that shown in [10c.].

It is worth noting that negative politeness is typically expressed via questions, even questions that seem to ask for permission to ask a question (for example, 'Might I ask …?') as in [10c.]. On the surface, such questions present an opportunity for the other to answer in the negative to the question without the same refusal effect of responding with a negative to a direct, bald on record imperative. (This distinction is an important motivation for the distinction between direct and indirect speech acts, discussed already.)

Even more relevant for our concern with the pragmatics of language in use, the availability of the bald on record form, as well as off record forms, means that the use of a face-saving on record form represents a significant choice. The choice of a type of expression that is less direct, potentially less clear, generally longer, and with a more complex structure means that the speaker is making a greater effort, in terms of concern for face (i.e. politeness), than is needed simply to get the basic message across efficiently.

These observations are summarized in Figure 7.1 overleaf.

Strategies

The tendency to use positive politeness forms, emphasizing closeness between speaker and hearer, can be seen as a **solidarity strategy**. This may be the principal operating strategy among a whole group or it may be an option used by an individual speaker on a particular occasion. Linguistically, such a strategy will include personal information, use of nicknames, sometimes even abusive terms (particularly among males), and shared dialect or slang expressions. Frequently, a solidarity strategy will be marked via inclusive terms such as 'we' and 'let's', as in the party invitation in [11].

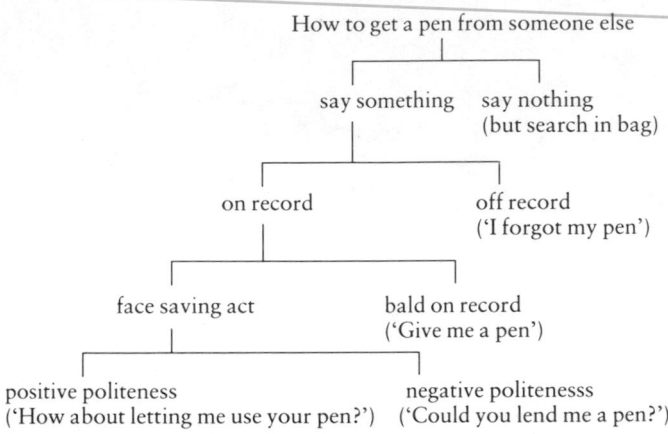

FIGURE 7.1 *How to get a pen from someone else (following Brown and Levinson 1987)*

[11] Come on, let's go to the party. Everyone will be there. We'll have fun.

The tendency to use negative politeness forms, emphasizing the hearer's right to freedom, can be seen as a **deference strategy**. It can be the typical strategy of a whole group or just an option used on a particular occasion. A deference strategy is involved in what is called 'formal politeness'. It is impersonal, as if nothing is shared, and can include expressions that refer to neither the speaker nor the hearer (for example, 'Customers may not smoke here, sir'). The language associated with a deference strategy emphasizes the speaker's and the hearer's independence, marked via an absence of personal claims, as in [12], an alternative version of the party invitation in [11].

[12] There's going to be a party, if you can make it. It will be fun.

These general types of strategies are illustrated here via utterances which are actually central to the speech event (for example, invitation). Face saving behavior, however, is often at work well before such utterances are produced, in the form of pre-sequences.

Pre-sequences

As already suggested, the concept of face saving may be helpful in understanding how participants in an interaction inevitably understand more than is said. The basic assumption, from the perspective of politeness, is that face is typically at risk when the self needs to accomplish something involving other. The greatest risk appears to be when the other is put in a difficult position. One way of avoiding risk is to provide an opportunity for the other to halt the potentially risky act. For example, rather than simply make a request, speakers will often first produce what can be described as a **pre-request**. We already noted one example in discussing speech events earlier, at the end of Chapter 6. Another is presented as [13], along with one analysis of the structure of this interaction.

[13] Her: Are you busy?   (= pre-request)
     Him: Not really.   (= go ahead)
     Her: Check over this memo.   (= request)
     Him: Okay.   (= accept)

The advantage of the pre-request element is that it can be answered either with a 'go-ahead' response, as in [13], or with a 'stop' response, as in [14].

[14] Him: Are you busy?   (= pre-request)
     Her: Oh, sorry.   (= stop)

The response in [14] allows the speaker to avoid making a request that cannot be granted at the time. Understanding that it is a response to a pre-request also allows us to interpret the expression 'sorry', not only as an apology about being busy, but also as an apology about being unable to respond to the anticipated request.

There is, however, a general pattern of pre-requests actually being treated as requests and being responded to, as in [15], with the (unstated, hoped for) action being performed.

[15] Her: Do you have a spare pen?
     Him: Here. (hands over a pen)

This 'short-cut' process of going from pre-request to granting of request helps explain the literal oddness of the common pattern in [16].

[16] Her: Do you mind if I use your phone?
Him: Yeah, sure.

As a literal response, 'Yeah' or 'Yeah, sure' would be the equivalent of 'I do mind' and wouldn't count as allowing use of the phone. However, these forms are normally interpreted as a positive response, not to the pre-request, but to the unstated request.

Pre-sequences are also commonly used in making invitations. As illustrated in [17], with a 'go ahead', and [18], with a 'stop', inviters tend to ask a **pre-invitation** question and receivers tend to recognize their function.

[17]	Him:	What are you doing this Friday?	(= pre-invitation)
	Her:	Hmm, nothing so far.	(= go ahead)
	Him:	Come over for dinner.	(= invitation)
	Her:	Oh, I'd like that.	(= accept)

[18]	Him:	Are you doing anything later?	(= pre-invitation)
	Her:	Oh, yeah. Busy, busy, busy.	(= stop)
	Him:	Oh, okay.	(= stop)

Children often use **pre-announcements** to check if their parents are willing to pay attention, as in example [19].

[19]	Child:	Mom, guess what happened?	(= pre-announcement)
	Mother:	(Silence)	
	Child:	Mom, you know what?	(= pre-announcement)
	Mother:	Not right now, Jacy, I'm busy.	(= stop)

In example [19], there are two pre-announcements, neither of which receives a 'go-ahead'. The initial pre-announcement is met with silence, which is generally interpreted as a 'stop'. The child's second attempt must be based on an interpretation that the parent did not hear the first attempt. The final response has to be interpreted as a 'stop', but noticeably it is expressed, in face-saving terms, as a postponement.

Throughout this discussion of politeness in interaction, we have been assuming a well-known and easily recognizable structure for the interaction. That structure must now be analyzed because it is our comfortable familiarity with its regularity that allows a great deal to be communicated that is never said.

8
Conversation and preference structure

The previous chapter focused on aspects of social awareness which can have an impact on what gets communicated by what is said during an interaction. The term 'interaction' could actually apply to a very large number of quite different social encounters. For example, a teacher talking to students in a classroom is one kind of interaction; others include a doctor talking to a patient in a clinic, or individuals taking part in courtroom proceedings, attending a committee meeting, buying stamps at the post office, and dozens of other different experiences people have in which there is interpersonal exchange of talk. The kind of talk is likely to differ according to the different contexts of interaction. However, the structure of the talk, the basic pattern of 'I speak—you speak—I speak—you speak', will derive from that fundamental kind of interaction we acquire first and use most often. This is the structure of conversation. Conversation structure is what we have been assuming as familiar throughout much of the preceding discussion. It is time to look more closely at that structure as a crucial aspect of pragmatics.

Conversation analysis

There are many metaphors used to describe conversation structure. For some, conversation is like a dance, with the conversational partners coordinating their movements smoothly. For others it's like traffic crossing an intersection, involving lots of alternating movement without any crashes. However, the most widely used analytic approach is based, not on dancing (there's no music) nor on traffic flow (there are no traffic signals), but on an analogy with the workings of a market economy.

In this market, there is a scarce commodity called the **floor** which can be defined as the right to speak. Having control of this scarce commodity at any time is called a **turn**. In any situation where control is not fixed in advance, anyone can attempt to get control. This is called **turn-taking**. Because it is a form of social action, turn-taking operates in accordance with a **local management system** that is conventionally known by members of a social group. The local management system is essentially a set of conventions for getting turns, keeping them, or giving them away. This system is needed most at those points where there is a possible change in who has the turn. Any possible change-of-turn point is called a **Transition Relevance Place**, or TRP. Within any social group, there will be features of talk (or absence of talk) typically associated with a TRP.

This type of analytic metaphor provides us with a basic perspective in which speakers having a conversation are viewed as taking turns at holding the floor. They accomplish change of turn smoothly because they are aware of the local management system for taking those turns at an appropriate TRP. The metaphor can be applied to those conversations where speakers cooperate and share the floor equally. It can also be used to describe those conversations where speakers seem to be in competition, fighting to keep the floor and preventing others from getting it. These patterns of conversational interaction differ substantially from one social group to another. In order to illustrate the system at work, we will focus on the conventions of one social group—middle class English speakers in public—while remaining aware that other social groups will have substantially different assumptions about the meaning of various features.

Pauses, overlaps, and backchannels

Most of the time, conversation consists of two, or more, participants taking turns, and only one participant speaking at any time. Smooth transitions from one speaker to the next seem to be valued. Transitions with a long silence between turns or with substantial **overlap** (i.e. both speakers trying to speak at the same time) are felt to be awkward. When two people attempt to have a conversation and discover that there is no 'flow', or smooth rhythm to their transitions, much more is being communicated than is said. There is a sense of distance, an absence of familiarity or ease, as in the interaction shown in [1] between a student and his friend's father during their first meeting.

[1] Mr. Strait: What's your major Dave?
    Dave: English—well I haven't really decided yet.
               (3 seconds)
    Mr. Strait: So—you want to be a teacher?
    Dave: No—not really—well not if I can help it.
               (2.5 seconds)
    Mr. Strait: Wha—// Where do you—   go ahead
    Dave: I mean it's a—oh sorry   // I em—

As shown in [1], very short pauses (marked with a dash) are simply hesitations, but longer pauses become silences. The silences in [1] are not attributable to either speaker because each has completed a turn. If one speaker actually turns over the floor to another and the other does not speak, then the silence is attributed to the second speaker and becomes significant. It's an **attributable silence**. As shown in [2], the non-response of Dave is treated, by his girlfriend, as possibly communicating something.

[2] Jan: Dave I'm going to the store.
           (2 seconds)
    Jan: Dave?
           (2 seconds)
    Jan: Dave—is something wrong?
    Dave: What? What's wrong?
    Jan: Never mind.

Silence at a TRP is not as problematic for the local management system as overlap. If the expectation is that only one person speaks at a time, then overlap can be a serious problem. Returning to example [1], the final two lines illustrate overlaps, conventionally marked by a double slash (//) at the beginning of the overlapping talk. Typically, the first overlap occurs as both speakers attempt to initiate talk. In accordance with the local management system, one speaker will stop to allow the other to have the floor. However, for two speakers who are having difficulty getting into a shared conversational rhythm, the stop-start-overlap-stop pattern may be repeated.

The type of overlap shown in [1] is simply part of a difficult first conversation with an unfamiliar person. There are other kinds of overlap and they are interpreted differently. For many (often younger) speakers, overlapped talk appears to function like an expression of solidarity or closeness in expressing similar opinions or values. As shown in [3], the effect of the overlapping talk creates a feeling of two voices collaborating as one, in harmony.

[3] Min: Did you see him in the video?
    Wendy: Yeah—the part on the beach
    Min: Oh my god // he was so sexy
    Wendy: he was just being so cool
    Min: And all the waves // crashing around him!
    Wendy: yeah that was really wild!

In example [3], overlap communicates closeness. In example [4], overlap communicates competition.

[4] Joe: when they were in
                // power las—   wait CAN I FINISH?
    Jerry: that's my point I said—

In example [4], the speakers may appear to be having a discussion, but they are, in fact, competing for the floor. The point at which overlap occurs is treated as an interruption and the first speaker actually has to make a comment about procedure (with a louder voice, shown by the capital letters in 'CAN I FINISH?') rather than about the topic of conversation.

By drawing attention to an expectation that he should be allowed to finish, the first speaker in [4] is appealing to some of the unstated 'rules' of conversation structure. Each potential speaker is expected to wait until the current speaker reaches a TRP. The most obvious markers of a TRP are the end of a structural unit (a phrase or clause) and a pause. Notice that, in [4], the first speaker has uttered 'when they were in—' at the point where the second speaker begins to talk. There is no pause and it is not the end of a phrase or clause. This is a clear interruption and breaks the 'rules'.

Normally, those who wish to get the floor will wait for a possible TRP before jumping in. Of course, those holding the floor in a competitive environment will avoid providing TRPs. To do so, they must avoid an open pause at the end of a syntactic unit. As illustrated in [5], the speaker fills each of his pauses ('um' or 'uh'), which are placed inside, not at the end of, syntactic units. (Just prior to this turn, another speaker had attempted to take the floor, so the speaker in [5] seems concerned to protect his turn.)

[5] I wasn't talking about—um his first book that was—uh really just like a start and so—uh isn't—doesn't count really.

Another type of floor-holding device is to indicate that there is a larger structure to your turn by beginning with expressions of the type shown in [6].

[6] a. There are three points I'd like to make—first …
b. There's more than one way to do this—one example would be …
c. Didn't you know about Melvin?—oh it was last October …
d. Did you hear about Cindy's new car?—she got it in …

The expressions in [6a.] and [6b.] are associated with discussions of facts or opinions whereas those in [6c.] and [6d.] are preludes to storytelling. In all cases, they are used to get the regular exchange of turn process suspended and allow one speaker to have an extended turn. Within an extended turn, however, speakers still expect their conversational partners to indicate that they are listening. There are many different ways of doing this, including head nods, smiles, and other facial expressions and gestures, but the most common vocal indications are called **backchannel signals**, or simply **backchannels**. Some of these are present in Mary's contributions to [7].

[7] Caller: if you use your long distance service a lot then you'll
Mary: uh-uh
Caller: be interested in the discount I'm talking about because
Mary: yeah
Caller: it can only save you money to switch to a cheaper service
Mary: mmm

These types of signals ('uh-uh', 'yeah', 'mmm') provide feedback to the current speaker that the message is being received. They normally indicate that the listener is following, and not objecting to, what the speaker is saying. Given this normal expectation, the absence of backchannels is typically interpreted as significant. During telephone conversations, the absence of backchannels may prompt the speaker to ask if the listener is still there. During face-to-face interaction, the absence of backchannels may be interpreted as a way of withholding agreement, leading to an inference of disagreement. In conversation, silence is significant and will be interpreted as meaningful.

Conversational style

Many of the features which characterize the turn-taking system of conversation are invested with meaning by their users. Even within a broadly defined community of speakers, there is often sufficient variation to cause potential misunderstanding. For example, some individuals expect that participation in a conversation will be very active, that speaking rate will be relatively fast, with almost no pausing between turns, and with some overlap or even completion of the other's turn. This is one **conversational style**. It has been called a **high involvement style**. It differs substantially from another style in which speakers use a slower rate, expect longer pauses between turns, do not overlap, and avoid interruption or completion of the other's turn. This non-interrupting, non-imposing style has been called a **high considerateness style**.

When a speaker who typically uses the first style gets into a conversation with a speaker who normally uses the second style, the talk tends to become one-sided. The active participation style will tend to overwhelm the other style. Neither speaker will necessarily recognize that it is the conversational styles that are slightly different. Instead, the more rapid-fire speaker may think the slower-paced speaker just doesn't have much to say, is shy, and perhaps boring or even stupid. In return, he or she is likely to be viewed as noisy, pushy, domineering, selfish, and even tiresome. Features of conversational style will often be interpreted as personality traits.

Adjacency pairs

Despite differences in style, most speakers seem to find a way to cope with the everyday business of social interaction. They are certainly helped in this process by the fact that there are many almost automatic patterns in the structure of conversation. Some clear examples are the greetings and goodbyes shown in [8] to [10].

[8] Anna: Hello. Bill: Hi.

[9] Anna: How are you? Bill: Fine.

[10] Anna: See ya! Bill: Bye.

These automatic sequences are called **adjacency pairs**. They always consist of a **first part** and a **second part**, produced by different speakers. The utterance of a first part immediately creates an expectation of the utterance of a second part of the same pair. Failure to produce the second part in response will be treated as a significant absence and hence meaningful. There is substantial variation in the forms which are used to fill the slots in adjacency pairs, as shown in [11], but there must always be two parts.

[11] First Part Second Part
    A: What's up? B: Nothin' much.
    A: How's it goin'? B: Jus' hangin' in there.
    A: How are things? B: The usual.
    A: How ya doin'? B: Can't complain.

The examples in [11] are typically found in the opening sequences of a conversation. Other types of adjacency pairs are illustrated in [12], including a question–answer sequence [12a.], a thanking–response [12b.], and a request–accept [12c.].

[12] First Part Second Part
    a. A: What time is it? B: About eight-thirty.
    b. A: Thanks. B: You're welcome.
    c. A: Could you help
        me with this? B: Sure.

Not all first parts immediately receive their second parts, however. It often happens that a question–answer sequence will be delayed while another question–answer sequence intervenes. The sequence will then take the form of Q1–Q2–A2–A1, with the middle pair (Q2–A2) being called an **insertion sequence**. Although there appears to be a question (Q2) in response to a question (Q1), the assumption is that once the second part (A2) of the insertion sequence is provided, the second part (A1) of the initial question (Q1) will follow. This pattern is illustrated in [13].

[13] Agent: Do you want the early flight?　(= Q1)
Client: What time does it arrive?　(= Q2)
Agent: Nine forty-five.　(= A2)
Client: Yeah—that's great.　(= A1)

An insertion sequence is one adjacency pair within another. Although the expressions used may be question–answer sequences, other forms of social action are also accomplished within this pattern. As shown in [14], there is a pair which consists of making a request—accepting the request (Q1–A1), with an insertion sequence of a question–answer pair (Q2–A2) which seems to function as a condition on the acceptance (A1) being provided.

[14] Jean: Could you mail this letter　(Q1 = Request)
for me?
Fred: Does it have a stamp on it?　(Q2)
Jean: Yeah.　(A2)
Fred: Okay.　(A1 = Acceptance)

The delay in acceptance in example [14], created by the insertion sequence, is one type of indication that not all first parts necessarily receive the kind of second parts the speaker might anticipate. Delay in response symbolically marks potential unavailability of the immediate (i.e. normally automatic) expected answer. Delay represents distance between what is expected and what is provided. Delay is always interpreted as meaningful. In order to see how delay is locally interpreted, we need some analytic terms for what is expected within certain types of adjacency pairs.

Preference structure

Adjacency pairs are not simply contentless noises in sequence. They represent social actions, and not all social actions are equal when they occur as second parts of some pairs. Basically, a first part that contains a request or an offer is typically made in the expectation that the second part will be an acceptance. An acceptance is structurally more likely than a refusal. This structural likelihood is called **preference**. The term is used to indicate a socially determined structural pattern and does not refer to any individual's mental or emotional desires. In this technical use of the word, preference is an observed pattern in talk and not a personal wish.

Preference structure divides second parts into **preferred** and **dispreferred** social acts. The preferred is the structurally expected next act and the dispreferred is the structurally unexpected next act. (The general patterns are presented in Table 8.1.)

First part	Second part	
	Preferred	Dispreferred
Assessment	agree	disagree
Invitation	accept	refuse
Offer	accept	decline
Proposal	agree	disagree
Request	accept	refuse

TABLE 8.1 *The general patterns of preferred and dispreferred structures (following Levinson 1983)*

In considering requests or offers as first parts, acceptance is the preferred and refusal is the dispreferred second part. In examples [15a.–d.], the responses in each second part all represent preferreds. Thus, acceptance or agreement is the preferred second part response to a request [15a.], an offer [15b.], an assessment [15c.], or a proposal [15d.].

[15]	First Part	Second Part
	a. Can you help me?	Sure.
	b. Want some coffee?	Yes, please.
	c. Isn't that really great?	Yes, it is.
	d. Maybe we could go for a walk.	That'd be great.

To get a sense of how expected these preferred second parts are in the examples in [15], imagine each of the first parts being met with silence. We might say that in any adjacency pair, silence in the second part is always an indication of a dispreferred response.

Indeed, silence often leads the first speaker to revise the first part in order to get a second part that is not silence from the other speaker. This may be clearer via an example, such as [16], where Jack's silence in response to Sandy's comment prompts Sandy to restate her assessment. Jack then agrees (a preferred) with Sandy's assessment.

[16] Sandy: But I'm sure they'll have good food there.
     (1.6 seconds)
  Sandy: Hmm—I guess the food isn't great.
  Jack: Nah—people mostly go for the music.

Notice that Jack's silence occurs where he would have had to produce a disagreement (i.e. a dispreferred response) regarding Sandy's assessment. Non-response communicates that the speaker is not in a position to provide the preferred response.

However, silence as a response is an extreme case, almost risking the impression of non-participation in the conversational structure. Generally speaking, when participants have to produce second part responses that are dispreferred, they indicate that they are doing something very marked.

In example [17], the first speaker has made a statement that the second speaker appears to disagree with. Agreement would be the preferred second part, eliciting a response such as 'Yeah' or even 'I think so'. The second speaker (Julie) finds herself in the position of producing a dispreferred.

[17] Cindy: So chiropodists do hands I guess.
  Julie: Em—well—out there—they they mostly work on
     people's feet.

Julie's dispreferred second part is marked with initial hesitations, as if it is difficult to perform this action (essentially correcting the other). There is a delay ('em', plus pause) in getting started and the actual statement which indicates disagreement only comes after a preface ('well'), an appeal to the views of others ('out there'), and a stumbling repetition ('they they'). Even the statement contains an expression ('mostly') which makes the information less challenging to the claim in the first part. The overall effect is that this speaker is presenting herself as having difficulty and is unwilling to have to say what is being stated.

Hesitations and prefaces are also found in dispreferred second parts to invitations, as shown in [18].

[18] Becky: Come over for some coffee later.
      Wally: Oh—eh—I'd love to—but you see—I—I'm
                supposed to get this finished—you know.

As is often the case, the expression of a refusal (a dispreferred second) can be accomplished without actually saying 'no'. Something that isn't said nevertheless gets communicated in [18]. After a preface ('Oh') and a hesitation ('eh'), the second speaker in [18] produces a kind of token acceptance ('I'd love to') to show appreciation of the invitation. Then, the other's understanding is invoked ('you see') and an account is presented ('I'm supposed to get this finished') to explain what prevents the speaker from accepting the invitation. There is also a meaning conveyed here that the speaker's circumstances are beyond his control because of an obligation ('I'm supposed to') and, once again, the inviter's understanding ('you know') is invoked.

The patterns associated with a dispreferred second in English are presented as a series of optional elements in [19].

[19] How to do a dispreferred	Examples
a. delay/hesitate	pause; er; em; ah
b. preface	well; oh
c. express doubt	I'm not sure; I don't know
d. token Yes	that's great; I'd love to
e. apology	I'm sorry; what a pity
f. mention obligation	I must do X; I'm expected in Y
g. appeal for understanding	you see; you know
h. make it non-personal	everybody else; out there
i. give an account	too much work; no time left
j. use mitigators	really; mostly; sort of; kinda
k. hedge the negative	I guess not; not possible

The overwhelming effect of a dispreferred is that more time and more language are used than in a preferred. More language essentially represents more distance between the end of the first part and the end of the second part. From a pragmatic perspective, the expression of a preferred (in response to an offer or invitation, for example) clearly represents closeness and quick connection. The expression of a dispreferred, as mapped out in [19], would represent distance and lack of connection. From a social perspective, it is easy to see why participants in a conversation might try to avoid creating contexts for dispreferreds. One obvious device for accomplishing this is to use those pre-sequences described at the end of Chapter 7. The best way to avoid a dispreferred second is not to get to the point where a first part of the pair is uttered. It must follow, then, that conversations between those who are close familiars will tend to have fewer elaborate dispreferreds than conversations between those who are still working out their social relationship. The amount of talk employed to accomplish a particular social action in conversation is a pragmatic indicator of the relative distance between the participants.

9
Discourse and culture

The emphasis in the preceding chapter was on the sequential structure of conversation, particularly on aspects of the turn-taking procedures for control of the floor, with less attention paid to what speakers had to say once they got the floor. Having gained the floor, speakers have to organize the structure and content of what they want to say. They have to package their messages in accordance with what they think their listeners do and do not know, as well as sequence everything in a coherent way. If those speakers decide to write out their messages, creating written text, they no longer have listeners providing immediate interactive feedback. Consequently, they have to rely on more explicit structural mechanisms for the organization of their texts. In this expanded perspective, speakers and writers are viewed as using language not only in its **interpersonal function** (i.e. taking part in social interaction), but also in its **textual function** (i.e. creating well-formed and appropriate text), and also in its **ideational function** (i.e. representing thought and experience in a coherent way). Investigating this much broader area of the form and function of what is said and written is called discourse analysis.

Discourse analysis

Discourse analysis covers an extremely wide range of activities, from the narrowly focused investigation of how words such as 'oh' or 'well' are used in casual talk, to the study of the dominant ideology in a culture as represented, for example, in its educational or political practices. When it is restricted to linguistic issues, discourse analysis focuses on the record (spoken or written) of the process by which language is used in some context to express intention.

Naturally, there is a great deal of interest in the structure of discourse, with particular attention being paid to what makes a well-formed text. Within this structural perspective, the focus is on topics such as the explicit connections between sentences in a text that create cohesion, or on elements of textual organization that are characteristic of storytelling, for example, as distinct from opinion expressing and other text types.

However, within the study of discourse, the pragmatic perspective is more specialized. It tends to focus specifically on aspects of what is unsaid or unwritten (yet communicated) within the discourse being analyzed. In order to do the pragmatics of discourse, we have to go beyond the primarily social concerns of interaction and conversation analysis, look behind the forms and structures present in the text, and pay much more attention to psychological concepts such as background knowledge, beliefs, and expectations. In the pragmatics of discourse, we inevitably explore what the speaker or writer has in mind.

Coherence

Generally, what language users have most in mind is an assumption of **coherence**, that what is said or written will make sense in terms of their normal experience of things. That 'normal' experience will be locally interpreted by each individual and hence will be tied to the familiar and the expected. In the neighborhood where I live, the notice in [1a.] means that someone is selling plants, but the notice in [1b.] does not mean that someone is selling garages.

[1] a. Plant Sale
     b. Garage Sale

Although these notices have an identical structure, they are interpreted differently. Indeed, the interpretation of [1b.], that someone is selling household items from their garage, is one that requires some familiarity with suburban life.

This emphasis on familiarity and knowledge as the basis of coherence is necessary because of evidence that we tend to make instant interpretations of familiar material and tend not to see possible alternatives. For example, the question presented in [2] is easily answered by many people.

[2] How many animals of each type did Moses take on the Ark?

If you immediately thought of 'two', then you accessed some common cultural knowledge, perhaps even without noticing that the name used ('Moses') was inappropriate. We actually create a coherent interpretation for a text that potentially does not have it.

We are also unlikely to stop and puzzle over 'a male and a female (what?)' as we read about the accident reported in [3].

[3] A motor vehicle accident was reported in front of Kennedy Theatre involving a male and a female.

We automatically 'fill in' details (for example, a male person driving one of the motor vehicles) to create coherence. We also construct familiar scenarios in order to make sense of what might first appear to be odd events, as in the newspaper headline in [4].

[4] Man Robs Hotel with Sandwich

If you created an interpretation for [4] that had the sandwich (perhaps in a bag) being used as if it was a gun, then you activated the kind of background knowledge expected by the writer (as confirmed by the rest of the newspaper article). You may, of course, have created a quite different kind of interpretation (for example, the man was eating the sandwich while robbing the hotel). Whatever it was, it was inevitably based on what you had in mind and not only on what was in the 'text' in [4].

Background knowledge

Our ability to arrive automatically at interpretations of the unwritten and the unsaid must be based on pre-existing knowledge structures. These structures function like familiar patterns from previous experience that we use to interpret new experiences. The most general term for a pattern of this type is a **schema** (plural, **schemata**). A schema is a pre-existing knowledge structure in memory.

If there is a fixed, static pattern to the schema, it is sometimes called a **frame**. A frame shared by everyone within a social group would be something like a prototypical version. For example, within a frame for an apartment, there will be assumed components such as kitchen, bathroom, and bedroom. The assumed elements of a frame are generally not stated, as in the advertisement in [5].

[5] Apartment for rent. $500. 763–6683.

A normal (local) interpretation of the small fragment of discourse in [5] will be based on not only an 'apartment' frame as the basis of inference (if X is an apartment, then X has a kitchen, a bathroom, and a bedroom), but also an 'apartment for rent' advertisement frame. Only on the basis of such a frame can the advertiser expect the reader to fill in 'per month' and not 'per year' after '$500' here. If a reader of the discourse in [5] expects that it would be 'per week', for example, then that reader clearly has a different frame (i.e. based on a different experience of the cost of apartment rental!). The pragmatic point will nevertheless be the same: the reader uses a pre-existing knowledge structure to create an interpretation of what is not stated in the text.

When more dynamic types of schemata are considered, they are more often described as scripts. A **script** is a pre-existing knowledge structure involving event sequences. We use scripts to build interpretations of accounts of what happened. For example, we have scripts for what normally happens in all kinds of events, such as going to a doctor's office, a movie theater, a restaurant, or a grocery store as in [6].

[6] I stopped to get some groceries but there weren't any baskets left so by the time I arrived at the check-out counter I must have looked like a juggler having a bad day.

Part of this speaker's normal script for 'getting groceries' obviously involves having a basket and going to the check-out counter. Everything else that happened in this event sequence is assumed to be shared background knowledge (for example, she went through a door to get inside the store and she walked around picking up items from shelves).

The concept of a script is simply a way of recognizing some expected sequence of actions in an event. Because most of the details of a script are assumed to be known, they are unlikely to be stated. For members of the same culture, the assumption of shared scripts allows much to be communicated that is not said. However, for members of different cultures, such an assumption can lead to a great deal of miscommunication.

Cultural schemata

Everyone has had the experience of surprise when some assumed component of an event is unexpectedly missing. I remember my first visit to a Moroccan restaurant and the absence of one of my 'restaurant script' requirements—there were no chairs! (The large comfortable cushions were an excellent replacement.) It is almost inevitable that our background knowledge structures, our schemata for making sense of the world, will be culturally determined. We develop our **cultural schemata** in the contexts of our basic experiences.

For some obvious differences (for example, cushions instead of chairs), we can readily modify the details of a cultural schema. For many other subtle differences, however, we often don't recognize that there may be a misinterpretation based on different schemata. In one reported example, an Australian factory supervisor clearly assumed that other factory workers would know that Easter was close and hence they would all have a holiday. He asked another worker, originally from Vietnam, about her plans, as in [7].

[7] You have five days off. What are you going to do?

The Vietnamese worker immediately interpreted the utterance in terms of being laid off (rather than having a holiday). Something good in one person's schema can sound like something bad in another's.

Cross-cultural pragmatics

The study of differences in expectations based on cultural schemata is part of a broad area of investigation generally known as **cross-cultural pragmatics**. To look at the ways in which meaning is constructed by speakers from different cultures will actually require a complete reassessment of virtually everything we have considered so far in this survey. The concepts and terminology may provide a basic analytic framework, but the realization of those concepts may differ substantially from the English language examples presented here.

When we reviewed the cooperative principle and the maxims, we assumed some kind of general middle-class Anglo-American cultural background. What if we assumed a cultural preference for *not* saying what you know to be the case in many situations? Such a preference is reported in many cultures and would clearly require a different approach to the relationship between the maxims of quality and quantity in a more comprehensive pragmatics.

When we considered turn-taking mechanisms, we did not explore the powerful role of silence within the normal conversational practices of many cultures. Nor did we include a discussion of a socially prescribed 'right to talk' which, in many cultures, is recognized as the structural basis of how interaction proceeds.

When we explored types of speech acts, we did not include any observations on the substantial differences that can exist cross-culturally in interpreting concepts like 'complimenting', 'thanking', or 'apologizing'. The typical American English style of complimenting creates great embarrassment for some Native American Indian receivers (it's perceived as excessive), and can elicit a reaction similar to apologizing from some Japanese receivers (it's perceived as impossible to accept). Indeed, it is unlikely that the division one cultural group makes between any two social actions such as 'thanking' or 'apologizing' will be matched precisely within another culture.

The study of these different cultural ways of speaking is sometimes called **contrastive pragmatics**. When the investigation focuses more specifically on the communicative behavior of non-native speakers, attempting to communicate in their second language, it is described as **interlanguage pragmatics**. Such studies increasingly reveal that we all speak with what might be called a **pragmatic accent**, that is, aspects of our talk that indicate what we assume is communicated without being said.

If we have any hope at all of developing the capacity for cross-cultural communication, we will have to devote a lot more attention to an understanding of what characterizes pragmatic accent, not only in others, but in ourselves. I hope that this brief survey has provided a beginning, and an incentive to explore further.

Readings

Chapter 1
Definitions and background

Text 1

GEORGIA GREEN: *Pragmatics and Natural Language Understanding.* Lawrence Erlbaum 1989, page 3

The broadest interpretation of pragmatics is that it is the study of understanding intentional human action. Thus, it involves the interpretation of acts assumed to be undertaken in order to accomplish some purpose. The central notions in pragmatics must then include belief, intention (or goal), plan, and act. Assuming that the means and/or the ends involve communication, pragmatics still encompasses all sorts of means of communication, including nonconventional, nonverbal, nonsymbolic ones as, for example, when a lifeguard throws a volleyball in the direction of a swimmer struggling in the ocean. The lifeguard believes that the swimmer wants assistance, and that the swimmer will understand that the volleyball thrown in his direction is intended (by the lifeguard) to be assistance, and that the swimmer will know how to take advantage of the volleyball's property of being lighter than water. That makes at least three beliefs and one intention on the part of the lifeguard, including two beliefs about the swimmer's beliefs, and one about the swimmer's desires.

▷ *From this description, it seems as if every act in life is part of pragmatics. Do you think that pragmatics is the study of all actions, or should it be limited to only certain actions? What kind of limitations would you propose?*

> ▷ *The final sentence in this brief extract mentions 'beliefs about … beliefs'. How can we know about a person's beliefs when we are analyzing their actions and utterances?*

> ▷ *If the swimmer doesn't want assistance (in the example), how does that affect the analysis?*

Text 2

'Pragmatics: meaning and context.' File 70 in *Language Files: Materials for an Introduction to Linguistics.* (6th edn.)
Ohio State University Press 1991, page 223

To fully understand the meaning of a sentence, we must also understand the context in which it was uttered. Consider the word *ball*. In a sentence such as, *He kicked the ball into the net*, we may visualize a round, black and white soccer ball about nine inches in diameter. In a sentence such as *She dribbled the ball down the court and shot a basket*, we would visualize a basket ball. Given yet another sentence, *She putted the ball in from two feet away*, we would visualize another ball, a golf ball. In these examples, the word *ball* is understood in different ways depending on what type of action is associated with it. Whatever understood meaning is common to *ball* in all of these contexts will be part of the word's core meaning. If we think of enough types of balls, we can come up with an invariant core meaning of *ball* that will allow speakers to refer to any ball in any context. Nevertheless, even though we can discover a word's 'invariant core', we normally understand more than this. It is the CONTEXT that fills in the details and allows full understanding—such as the usual color of a soccer ball, the size of a basketball, or the weight of a golf ball. The study of the contribution of context to meaning is often called pragmatics.

> ▷ *What do you think is the 'invariant core' meaning of the word 'ball', as proposed here? Can you think of any use of the word 'ball' that would not have that 'core' meaning? Can 'the context' cause a word not to have its 'core' meaning?*

> ▷ *What does the term 'context' seem to refer to in this text? If you have a different concept of 'context', how would you revise this paragraph to illustrate it more clearly?*

> *In what ways is the view of pragmatics in this text similar to or different from the way pragmatics is defined in Text 1?*

Chapter 2
Deixis and distance

Text 3

CHARLES FILLMORE: *Santa Cruz Lectures on Deixis.*
Indiana University Linguistics Club 1975, pages 40–2

The most obvious place deictic terms in English are the adverbs 'here' and 'there' and the demonstratives 'this' and 'that', along with their plural forms; the most obvious time deictic words are adverbs like 'now' or 'today'. There are important distinctions in the uses of these and other deictic words which I would like us to be clear about right away. I will frequently need to point out whether a word or expression that I am referring to can be used in one or more of three different ways, and these I will call *gestural*, *symbolic*, and *anaphoric*. By the *gestural* use of a deictic expression I mean that use by which it can be properly interpreted only by somebody who is monitoring some physical aspect of the communication situation; by the *symbolic* use of a deictic expression I mean that use whose interpretation involves merely knowing certain aspects of the speech communication situation, whether this knowledge comes by current perception or not; and by the *anaphoric* use of an expression I mean that use which can be correctly interpreted by knowing what other portion of the same discourse the expression is *coreferential* with.

I can illustrate the distinction I'm talking about by taking the word 'there'. It has all three uses. Its gestural use can be seen in a sentence like, 'I want you to put it there'. You have to know where the speaker is pointing in order to know what place he is indicating. The symbolic use is exemplified in the telephoner's utterance, 'Is Johnny there?'. This time we understand the word 'there' as meaning 'in the place where you are'. An example of the anaphoric use of 'there' is a sentence like 'I drove the car to the parking lot and left it there'. In that case the word refers to a place which had been identified earlier in the discourse, namely the parking lot. Take another example, this time one showing just the distinction between the gestural and the symbolic use. If during my lecture you hear me use a phrase like 'this finger', the chances are fairly good that you will look up to see what it is that I want you to see; you will expect the word to be accompanied by a gesture or demonstration of some sort. On the other hand, if you hear me use the phrase 'this campus', you do not need to look up, because you know my meaning to be 'the campus in which I am now located', and you happen to know where I am. The former is the gestural use, the latter the symbolic use.

> ▷ *Can you transfer this discussion to temporal deixis (as described in Chapter 2), considering 'then' (instead of 'there') in gestural, symbolic, and anaphoric uses?*

> ▷ *Given the three categories described here, which category seems to fit the typical uses of deictic expressions such as 'yesterday' and 'tomorrow'?*

Place indications take part in the deictic system of a language by virtue of the fact that for many locating expressions, the location of one, or another, or both, of the speech act participants can serve as a spatial reference point. Sometimes all that means is that for an expression which in a nondeictic use requires mention of a reference object, in its deictic use the reference object, taken to be the speaker's body at the time of the speech act, simply goes unmentioned. Take, for example, the expression 'upstairs'. If I say, 'Johnny lives upstairs', you will understand me as meaning upstairs of the place where I am at the time I say the sentence, unless the immediately preceding discourse has provided some other reference point. If I say 'Harry lives nearby', the same can be said. You will understand that Harry lives near to the place where I am when I say the sentence, again, except for the case where a reference point has been identified in the immediately preceding discourse.

> ▷ *Is the speaker's body always the unmentioned reference point, as Fillmore suggests here? Consider the uses of words like 'front', 'back', 'down (the street)', 'above', 'outside', and any others that seem to be similar to 'upstairs' and 'nearby' in the examples.*

Text 4

QUENTIN SMITH: 'The multiple uses of indexicals' in
Synthese 78, 1989, pages 182–3

'I am in last place' is often used to indicate that the speaker is in last place. But this sentence is also used on a number of occasions to indicate that somebody else is in last place. I am watching a race and the person upon whom I have bet, No. 10, drops to the last place. 'I am in last place!' I exclaim in anguish to my companion. My companion knows perfectly well what I mean—that *the person upon whom I have bet* is in last place. Indeed, she replies in kind, disagreeing with my statement. 'No you aren't! Look!' she exclaims, pointing at No. 10, 'You are passing No. 3!'

▷ *Can you think of any other contexts where 'I' is not to be literally interpreted as 'the person who is speaking'?*

▷ *Do examples such as these mean that we need a new definition of the meaning of the word 'I' in English? If yes, what would have to be in that definition? If no, how would you explain this type of 'extra' usage?*

Text 5

GEOFFREY NUNBERG: 'Indexicality and deixis' in
Linguistics and Philosophy 16, 1993, page 41

... you might point at a picture of John Ashberry to identify his most recent book, using the demonstrative that, with no restriction on the things you could say about it:

(94) That is in all the bookstores (on the top shelf, temporarily out of stock).

But while John Ashberry might easily say of himself 'I am in all the bookstores,' it would be odd for him to say 'I am on the top shelf' or 'I am temporarily out of stock,' unless it could be supposed that the fact that an author's book was on the top shelf or was temporarily out of stock carried some noteworthy implications for him.

▷ *Following on from these examples, could you point to an empty space on the bookshelf and and ask the owner of the bookstore, 'Is that out of stock?'? If yes, do we have to reformulate the definition of deixis (i.e. 'pointing via language') when there's nothing being pointed to?*

▷ Why do you think the idea of 'some noteworthy implications' is mentioned in this text? Does identifying the reference of deictic expressions depend on information about a person's thoughts and feelings? If yes, can you think of other examples (involving other deictic forms)?

▷ How does the example with 'I' in this text fit in with your analysis of 'I' in Text 4?

Chapter 3
Reference and inference

Text 6

KEITH DONNELLAN: 'Reference and definite descriptions' in *Philosophical Review* 75, 1966, pages 285–6

I will call the two uses of definite descriptions I have in mind the attributive use and the referential use. A speaker who uses a definite description attributively in an assertion states something about whoever or whatever is the so-and-so. A speaker who uses a definite description referentially in an assertion, on the other hand, uses the description to enable his audience to pick out whom or what he is talking about and states something about that person or thing. In the first case the definite description might be said to occur essentially, for the speaker wishes to assert something about whatever or whoever fits that description; but in the referential use the definite description is merely one tool for doing a certain job—calling attention to a person or thing—and in general any other device for doing the same job, another description or a name, would do as well. In the attributive use, the attribute of being the so-and-so is all important, while it is not in the referential use.

To illustrate this distinction, in the case of a single sentence, consider the sentence, 'Smith's murderer is insane.' Suppose first that we come upon poor Smith foully murdered. From the brutal manner of the killing and the fact that Smith was the most lovable person in the world, we might exclaim, 'Smith's murderer is insane.' I will assume, to make it a simpler case, that in a quite ordinary sense we do not know who murdered Smith (though this is not in the end essential to the case). This, I shall say, is an attributive use of the definite description.

The contrast with such a use of the sentence is one of those situations in which we expect and intend our audience to realize whom we have in mind when we speak of Smith's murderer and, most importantly, to know that it is this person about whom we are going to say something.

▷ *Before Donnellan's proposal, many philosophers argued that if a description does not fit anything, then it fails to refer. What is Donnellan's perspective on this?*

▷ *Using Donnellan's distinction (plus any additional distinctions you think are needed), how would you account for the use of a definite description that does not accurately fit the person or thing?*

▷ *Can the attributive versus referential distinction be related to Fillmore's distinction (Text 3) between gestural, symbolic, and anaphoric uses of deictic expressions?*

Text 7

M.A.K.HALLIDAY and RUQAIYA HASAN: *Cohesion in English*. Longman 1976, page 31

There are certain items in every language which have the property of reference, in the specific sense in which we are using the term here; that is to say, instead of being interpreted semantically in their own right, they make reference to something else for their interpretation. In English these items are personals, demonstratives and comparatives.

We start with an example of each:

a. Three blind mice, three blind mice.
   See how they run! See how they run!

b. Doctor Foster went to Gloucester in a shower of rain.
   He stepped in a puddle right up to his middle and never went there again.

c. There were two wrens upon a tree.
   Another came, and there were three.

In (a), *they* refers to *three blind mice*; in (b) *there* refers to *Gloucester*; in (c) *another* refers to *wrens*.

These items are directives indicating that information is to be retrieved from elsewhere. So much they have in common with all cohesive elements. What characterizes this particular type of cohesion, that which we are calling REFERENCE, is the specific nature of the information that is signalled for retrieval. In the case of reference the information to be retrieved is the referential meaning, the identity of the particular thing or class of things that is being referred to; and the cohesion lies in the continuity of reference, whereby the same thing enters into the discourse a second time.

▷ *In this analysis, the assumption is that certain words refer to other words. Do you think that this is a helpful or misleading assumption?*

▷ *Do you agree with the final statement that 'the same thing enters into the discourse a second time'? How about example (c), where the analysis proposes that the word 'another' refers to 'wrens'?*

▷ *If the word 'there' in (b) is an example of cohesion by reference, is the word 'there' in the second line of (c) the same? How do you decide?*

▷ *Is Donnellan's distinction in Text 6 relevant to what these authors are saying?*

Chapter 4
Presupposition and entailment

Text 8
ROBERT C. STALNAKER: 'Pragmatic presupposition' in Milton Munitz and Peter Unger (eds.): *Semantics and Philosophy*. New York University Press 1974, pages 199–200

Although it is normally inappropriate because unnecessary for me to assert something that each of us assumes the other already believes, my assertions will of course always have consequences which are part of the common background. For example, in a context where we both know that my neighbor is an adult male,

I say 'My neighbor is a bachelor,' which, let us suppose, entails that he is adult and male. I might just as well have said 'my neighbor is unmarried.' The same information would have been conveyed (although the nuances might not have been exactly the same). That is, *the increment of information*, or of content, conveyed by the first statement is the same as that conveyed by the second. If the asserted proposition were accepted, and added to the common background, the resulting situation would be the same as if the second assertion were accepted and added to the background.

This notion of common background belief is the first approximation to the notion of pragmatic presupposition that I want to use. A proposition P is a pragmatic presupposition of a speaker in a given context just in case the speaker assumes or believes that P, assumes or believes that his addressee assumes or believes that P, and assumes or believes that his addressee recognizes that he is making these assumptions, or has these beliefs.

▷ *Do you agree that the two utterances quoted in the first paragraph would add exactly the same information to the common background?*

▷ *According to the definition presented in the second paragraph, would it be correct, or not, to say that a pragmatic presupposition is any belief of the speaker? (It may be helpful to look again at Chapter 4, pages 25–30.)*

▷ *Can you think of circumstances where it is not inappropriate for someone 'to assert something that each of us assumes the other already believes'?*

Text 9

GERALD GAZDAR: *Pragmatics. Implicature, Presupposition, and Logical Form.* Academic Press 1979, page 106

(65) *John got to safety before the boiler blew up.*
(66) *John got to the safety handle before the boiler blew up.*

If we assume in (66) that John's getting to the safety handle prevented the boiler blowing up, then (66) does not, but (65) does, presuppose that the boiler blew up. If we treat *before* as being 'ambiguous', then we are again left with no principle for deciding whether or not the presupposition attaches to a particular sentence. Note also that, if all presupposing constructions are ambiguous, then the notion of 'infelicity' or 'unacceptability' is inapplicable, since we will always have an alternative reading with respect to which the sentence will be acceptable.

▷ *How do you account for the fact that 'before' creates a presupposition in example (65), but not in (66)? Can you think of other examples where the use of 'before' does, or does not, lead to a presupposition?*

▷ *Does 'after' work the same way? Should we define 'before' and 'after', not only as opposites, but also as creating different presuppositions?*

Chapter 5
Cooperation and implicature

Text 10
PAUL GRICE: 'Logic and conversation' in P. Cole and J. L. Morgan (eds.): *Syntax and Semantics Volume 3: Speech Acts.* Academic Press 1975, page 48

I would like to be able to think of the standard type of conversational practice not merely as something that all or most do IN FACT follow but as something that it is REASONABLE for us to follow, that we SHOULD NOT abandon. For a time, I was attracted by the idea that observance of the CP [co-operative principle] and the maxims, in a talk exchange, could be thought of as a quasi-contractual matter, with parallels outside the realm of discourse. If you pass by when I am struggling with my stranded car, I no doubt have some degree of expectation that you will offer help, but once you join me in tinkering under the hood, my expectations become stronger and take more specific forms (in the absence of indications that you are merely an incompetent meddler); and talk exchanges seemed to me to exhibit, characteristically, certain features that jointly distinguish cooperative transactions:

1. The participants have some common immediate aim, like getting a car mended; their ultimate aims may, of course, be

independent and even in conflict—each may want to get the car mended in order to drive off, leaving the other stranded. In characteristic talk exchanges, there is a common aim even if, as in an over-the-wall chat, it is a second order one, namely that each party should, for the time being, identify himself with the transitory conversational interests of the other.

2. The contributions of the participants should be dovetailed, mutually dependent.

3. There is some sort of understanding (which may be explicit but which is often tacit) that, other things being equal, the transaction should continue in appropriate style unless both parties are agreeable that it should terminate. You do not just shove off or start doing something else.

But while some such quasi-contractual basis as this may apply to some cases, there are too many types of exchange, like quarreling and letter writing, that it fails to fit comfortably.

▷ *Can you spell out why 'quarreling and letter writing' do not fit comfortably with the conditions presented here?*

▷ *What would you call the three 'features' listed here if you were to make them into maxims for cooperative transactions?*

▷ *Grice emphasizes the word 'reasonable' as he describes his consideration of the cooperative principle and his maxims as a kind of contract. Would the cooperative principle, the maxims, and the three features listed here be treated as 'reasonable' in all societies and cultures?*

Text 11
J. L. MORGAN: 'Two types of convention in indirect speech acts' in P. Cole (ed.): *Syntax and Semantics Volume 9: Pragmatics.* Academic Press 1978, pages 277–8

Just above I presented cases involving particular expressions and the conventionalization of their use for certain implicatures, as in the case of *If you've seen one, you've seen them all*, or the original example, *Can you pass the salt?* I said in the latter case that it had become a convention of usage to use this expression, with its literal meaning, to convey an implicature of request. The question now arises, can there be this kind of conventionalization of rules of conversation? I think there can. For example, it is more or less conventional to challenge the wisdom of a suggested course of action by questioning the mental health of the suggestor, by ANY appropriate linguistic means, as in:

(37) *Are you crazy?*
(38) *Have you lost your mind?*
(39) *Are you out of your gourd?*

and so on. Most Americans have two or three stock expressions usable as answers to obvious questions, as in:

(40) *Is the Pope Catholic?*
(41) *Do bagels wear bikinis?*

But for some speakers the convention does not specify a particular expression, and new ones are manufactured as they are needed. It seems that here a schema for implicature has been conventionalized: Answer an obvious yes/no question by replying with another question whose answer is very obvious and the same as the answer you intend to convey.

In a similar way, most speakers have a small number of expressions usable as replies to assertions, with the implicature that the assertion is transparently false—(42), for example:

(42) *Yes, and I'm Marie the Queen of Romania.*

But again, for some speakers the convention specifies only a general strategy, rather than a particular expression: To convey that an assertion is transparently false, reply with another assertion even more transparently false.

▷ *Do you know any other 'stock expressions' for these types of occasions (request, challenge, answer to obvious questions, reply to a false assertion)? How would you explain (to someone learning English as a foreign language, for example) how to work out the communicated meaning from the literal meaning?*

▷ *The author uses the term 'convention' in talking about the kinds of implicatures involved here. Do you think that the examples presented here can be analyzed in terms of conventional implicatures (as discussed in Chapter 5, pages 45–6)?*

▷ *What do you think about the idea that an implicature may begin by being based on inference, but can become so conventionalized that no one has to make the inference any more? Is that the same process as we use in interpreting idioms?*

Chapter 6
Speech acts and events

Text 12
JOHN SEARLE: *Speech Acts*. Cambridge University Press 1969, pages 58–9

One crucial distinction between promises on the one hand and threats on the other is that a promise is a pledge to do something for you, not to you; but a threat is a pledge to do something to you, not for you. A promise is defective if the thing promised is something the promisee does not want done; and it is further defective if the promisor does not believe the promisee wants it done, since a non-defective promise must be intended as a promise and not as a threat or warning. Furthermore, a promise, unlike an invitation, normally requires some sort of occasion or situation that calls for the promise. A crucial feature of such occasions or situations seems to be that the promisee wishes (needs, desires, etc.) that something be done, and the promisor is aware of this wish (need, desire, etc.). I think both halves of this double condition are necessary in order to avoid fairly obvious counter-examples.

▷ *This paragraph lists several required features for a speech act to count as a promise. Do you agree that all these features are necessary? Are other crucial features not included here?*

One can, however, think of apparent counter-examples to this condition as stated. Suppose I say to a lazy student, 'If you don't hand in your paper on time I promise you I will give you a failing grade in the course'. Is this utterance a promise? I am inclined to think not; we would more naturally describe it as a warning or possibly even a threat. But why, then, is it possible to use the locution 'I promise' in such a case? I think we use it here because 'I promise' and 'I hereby promise' are among the strongest illocutionary force indicating devices for *commitment* provided by the English language. For that reason we often use these expressions in the performance of speech acts which are not strictly speaking promises, but in which we wish to emphasize the degree of our commitment. To illustrate this, consider another apparent counter-example to the analysis along different lines. Sometimes one hears people say 'I promise' when making an emphatic assertion. Suppose, for example, I accuse you of having stolen the money. I say, 'You stole that money, didn't you?'. You reply, 'No, I didn't, I promise you I didn't'. Did you make a promise in this case? I find it very unnatural to describe your utterance as a promise. This utterance would be more aptly described as an emphatic denial, and we can explain the occurrence of the illocutionary force indicating device 'I promise' as derivative from genuine promises and serving here as an expression adding emphasis to your denial.

▷ *Do you agree that having used the words 'I promise', you could later claim that 'strictly speaking' you did not make a promise because you meant something else?*

▷ *What seem to be the conditions for an utterance containing the IFID 'I promise' to serve as an emphatic denial?*

▷ *Is the recognition of speech act conditions related at all to the cooperative principle as discussed in Text 10? (It may be helpful to refer to the discussion of felicity conditions in Chapter 6, pages 50–1.)*

Text 13
GEOFFREY LEECH: *Principles of Pragmatics.*
Longman 1983, pages 177–8

In referring to human conversational behavior, as to other areas of experience, our language provides us with categorical distinctions. But it is to commit a fundamental and obvious error to assume that the distinctions made by our vocabulary necessarily exist in reality. Language provides us with verbs like *order, request, beg, plead*, just as it provides us with nouns like *puddle, pond, lake, sea, ocean*. But we should no more assume that there are in pragmatic reality distinct categories such as orders and requests than that there are in geographical reality distinct categories such as puddles, ponds and lakes. Somehow, this assumption slips unnoticed into Searle's introduction to his taxonomy:

> What are the criteria by which we can tell that of three actual utterances one is a report, one a prediction and one a promise? In order to develop higher order genera, we must first know how the species *promise, prediction, report,* etc. differ from one another.
> (Searle, J. 1979.: *Expression and Meaning.* Cambridge: Cambridge University Press, page 2.)

But it would be strikingly inappropriate if one were to begin a treatise on expanses of water on the world's surface in this way:

> What are the criteria by which we can tell that of three actual expanses of water, one is a puddle, one a pond, and one a lake? In order to develop higher order genera, we must first know how the species *puddle, pond,* and *lake* differ from one another.

In defence of Searle it could be argued, first, that the comparison is unfair: if one had chosen monkeys and giraffes (say) instead of ponds and puddles, the example would have been less ridiculous. But my reply is (a) that one has no right *in advance* to assume that such categories exist in reality (although one might discover them by observation); and (b) that in actuality, when one *does* observe them, illocutions are in many respects more like puddles and ponds than like monkeys and giraffes: they are, that is to say, distinguished by continuous rather than by discrete characteristics.

▷ *What exactly is the argument being presented here against the idea that we can identify a speech act as a prediction or not?*

▷ *What would distinguish the definition of a puddle, in Leech's view, from the kind of definition of a promise presented in Text 12?*

▷ *Do you think that Leech's argument is based on an important issue, or just a minor point? How do you think Searle would respond to this criticism from Leech?*

Text 14

ROBIN LAKOFF: *Talking Power. The Politics of Language.*
Basic Books 1990, pages 34, 36, 38

Indirectness can function as a form of politeness. Politeness is a system of interpersonal relations designed to facilitate interaction by minimizing the potential for conflict and confrontation inherent in all human interchange. We like to think of conversation as conflict-free, with speakers normally being able to satisfy one another's needs and interests. But, in fact, we enter every conversation—indeed, every kind of discourse—with some personal desideratum in mind: perhaps as obvious as a favor or as subtle as the desire to be likeable. For some of these needs, participants can accede to each other, and both gain their desires; but with others, one must lose, however minimally, for the other to win. One person must tell another something that the other doesn't want to hear; one person must refuse another's request; one person must end a conversation before the other is quite willing to go. In such cases, there is the danger of insult and, consequently, the breakdown of communication. If societies did not devise ways to smooth over moments of conflict and confrontation, social relationships would be difficult to establish and continue, and essential cohesion would erode. Politeness strategies are the means to preserve at least the semblance of harmony and cohesion. ...

▷ *In what ways is this definition of politeness more or less specific than the general social meaning of politeness you are familiar with?*

Distancing cultures weave remoteness into their language. The attribution of responsibility represents an intrusion of the personal: it suggests that individuals with different interests are involved in the discussion. So grammatical devices that minimize a speaker's personal involvement are favored—for instance, passive verb forms and impersonal forms like *one*. Words that threaten to convey or evoke dangerous emotion are replaced with safer ones, which suggest that no emotion is involved. This formal language is the language of diplomacy, bureaucracy, and the professions. Diplomats speak of an *incident* when they mean that their countries are in a virtual state of war; bureaucrats talk of *revenue enhancement* when they renege on a promise of no new taxes; doctors discourse on *iatrogenesis* when they mean they did something that made the patient sick. These words provide a buffer between pure denotative meaning and its emotional wallop: the hearer, in all probability, knows perfectly well what the speaker intends; but the latter has chosen deliberately Latinate words from a sector of the vocabulary not rich in emotional connotations, so as to lessen the danger of collision.

▷ *Can you think of other examples of distance politeness in language use?*

▷ *Can you think of situations or special circumstances where the type of distance politeness, as defined here, is ignored?*

It is essential to realize that camaraderie can be conventional ... . But ... someone unaccustomed to conventional camaraderie will take it as genuine, arising out of long acquaintance and the development of mutual liking and trust. Modern camaraderie probably began in California as an outgrowth of the human potential movement of the 1960s and 1970s. For a while it was a bane to visiting Easterners, who were confounded by the Californian's appearance of good fellowship and deep caring; the immediate first-naming, touching, looking deep into the eyes, and asking *truly caring* questions: 'Are you really happy with your life?' To the properly brought-up Easterner, such behavior was permissible only after years of earning it, and maybe not then. Easterners fell into one of several schools of thought about the character of Californians: either that they had the simplicity of children and should be patronized; or that they were rough frontier sorts, probably raised by wolves (and you know how wolves are); or that they were truly wonderful people who could get to know you as well after two seconds as would take most of us a lifetime. All of these attitudes assumed, of course, that the camaraderie was real rather than conventional.

▷ *What examples of language use would you predict (or have you experienced) as representative of 'conventional camaraderie' in contrast to 'distance politeness'?*

Text 15

GABRIELE KASPER: 'Politeness' in R. E. Asher (ed.):
The Encyclopedia of Language and Linguistics. Volume 6.
Pergamon 1994, page 3209

Some types of linguistic action are carried out more frequently in some cultures than in others. Hearer-beneficial acts such as complimenting and thanking occur more regularly in some Western contexts (e.g., the USA) than in some Asian cultures (e.g., mainland China), reflecting both the strong positive politeness orientation and reluctance to impose on others in mainstream American culture, on the one hand, and the assumption, in China, that participants act according to their social positions and associated roles and obligations, on the other. Also, hearer-costly acts such as refusals are perceived as being more socially offensive by Japanese and Chinese interlocutors and thus tend to be avoided, whereas it seems more consistent with American interlocutors' right to self-determination not to comply with another person's wishes.

▷ *Can you think of other 'hearer-beneficial acts' and other 'hearer-costly acts'? For example, what is an invitation or a complaint? Is it possible that the concepts of 'cost' and 'benefit' may be culturally determined?*

▷ *There is a suggestion in this text that people in the USA are more concerned with their rights as individuals than with their social roles and obligations. What kind of evidence from language behavior would you look for in order to decide whether this suggestion is true or not?*

▷ *Can you characterize the normal behavior of your own social group as having more 'hearer-beneficial' acts? What about 'hearer-costly' acts? Are there other social groups with whom you share the same language, but whose politeness strategies appear to be different?*

▷ *Where does Lakoff's 'conventional camaraderie' (Text 14) fit into the distinction that Kasper is making here?*

PENELOPE BROWN and STEPHEN LEVINSON: *Politeness.*
Cambridge University Press 1987, page 281

In language the constraints are more on form than on content (or
at least form provides a more feasible area of study). The ways in
which messages are hedged, hinted, made deferential, and embed-
ded in discourse structures then become crucial areas of study. But
such areas are also the concern of pragmatics, the study of the
systematic relation of a language to context. The special interest
of sociolinguistics in our view is in the differential use of such
pragmatic resources by different categories of speakers in different situations. It is in this way that we derive our slogan
'Sociolinguistics should be applied pragmatics.'

▷ *Do you agree with the assumption that pragmatics comes first
and then is 'applied' to the social use of language, or should it
be the other way round?*

▷ *Notice that the concepts of 'hedge' and 'hint' are used here.
Recall the use of 'hedges' on implicatures in Chapter 5, pages
38–9 (which themselves may be termed 'hints'); would such
phenomena in the use of language be better analyzed as
aspects of politeness? Is pragmatics really just the study of linguistic politeness?*

▷ *Does the 'slogan' at the end of this text provide a better (or
worse) perspective on pragmatics than those offered in Texts
1 and 2 earlier?*

Chapter 8
Conversation and preference structure

Text 17
HARVEY SACKS: *Lectures on Conversation.* Volume 1.
Blackwell 1992, pages 3–4

I'll start off by giving some quotations.

    (1) A: Hello.
          B: Hello.
    (2) A: This is Mr Smith may I help you.
          B: Yes, this is Mr Brown.

(3) A: This is Mr Smith may I help you.
   B: I can't hear you.
   A: This is Mr <u>Smith</u>.
   B: Smith.

These are some first exchanges in telephone conversations collected at an emergency psychiatric hospital. They are occurring between persons who haven't talked to each other before. One of them, A, is a staff member of this psychiatric hospital. B can be either somebody calling about themselves, that is to say in trouble in one way or another, or somebody calling about somebody else.

I have a large collection of these conversations, and I got started looking at these first exchanges as follows. A series of persons who called this place would not give their names. The hospital's concern was, can anything be done about it? One question I wanted to address was, where in the course of the conversation could you tell that somebody would not give their name? So I began to look at the materials. It was in fact on the basis of that question that I began to try to deal in detail with conversations.

I found something that struck me as fairly interesting quite early. And that was that if the staff member used 'This is Mr Smith may I help you' as their opening line, then overwhelmingly, any answer other than 'Yes, this is Mr Brown' (for example, 'I can't hear you,' 'I don't know,' 'How do you spell your name?') meant that you would have serious trouble getting the caller's name, if you got the name at all. ...

Looking at the first exchange compared to the second, we can be struck by two things. First of all, there seems to be a fit between what the first person who speaks uses as their greeting, and what the person who is given that greeting returns. So that if A says, 'Hello,' then B tends to say 'Hello.' If A says 'This is Mr Smith may I help you,' B tends to say 'Yes, this is Mr Brown.' We can say there's a procedural rule there, that a person who speaks first in a telephone conversation can choose their form of address, and in choosing their form of address they can thereby choose the form of address the other uses.

▷ *Do you think that the 'procedural rule' presented here applies to all 'first exchanges' in telephone conversations?*

▷ *Can you describe this 'procedural rule' in terms of preference structure (as outlined in Chapter 8, pages 78–82) by including example (3) in your analysis?*

▷ *What advantages and disadvantages do you think there are in using telephone data as the basis for analyzing how conversation works?*

Text 18

H. SACKS, E. SCHEGLOFF, and G. JEFFERSON: 'A simplest systematics for the organization of turn-taking in conversation' in *Language* 50, 1974, pages 700–1

To merit serious consideration, it seems to us, a model should be capable of accommodating (i.e., either be compatible with, or allow the derivation of) the following grossly apparent facts. In any conversation, we observe the following:

(1) Speaker-change recurs, or at least occurs.
(2) Overwhelmingly, one party talks at a time.
(3) Occurrences of more than one speaker at a time are common, but brief.
(4) Transitions (from one turn to a next) with no gap and no overlap are common. Together with transitions characterized by slight gap or slight overlap, they make up the vast majority of transitions.
(5) Turn order is not fixed, but varies.
(6) Turn size is not fixed, but varies.
(7) Length of conversation is not specified in advance.
(8) What parties say is not specified in advance.
(9) Relative distribution of turns is not specified in advance.
(10) Number of parties can vary.
(11) Talk can be continuous or discontinous.
(12) Turn-allocation techniques are obviously used. A current speaker may select a next speaker (as when he addresses a question to another party); or parties may self-select in starting to talk.
(13) Various 'turn-constructional units' are employed; e.g., turns can be projectedly 'one word long', or they can be sentential in length.
(14) Repair mechanisms exist for dealing with turn-taking errors and violations; e.g., if two parties find themselves

talking at the same time, one of them will stop prematurely, thus repairing the trouble.

▷ *Can you divide these fourteen statements into two groups—one that applies to all conversations and one that applies to only some conversations in some contexts? What kinds of situations or people appear to create exceptions?*

▷ *Should these statements be restricted to any conversation that is middle-class American and basically friendly? Can you think of different factors such as social class, culture, ethnicity, relationship, age—or any others that will have an effect on how turn-taking proceeds?*

Text 19
JACK BILMES: *Discourse and Behavior.* Plenum Press 1986, page 166

Consider the following exchange:

A [addressing B]: Where are you going?
B [no response]
A The hell with you.

This exchange makes sense. It is orderly, not random. We may characterize B's (non)response with an infinite variety of negatives. It is not a question, not a promise, not a lecture, and so forth. However, given that questions call for answers, it is *relevantly* not an answer.

▷ *Why do you think the word 'relevantly' is emphasized in this text? Does this mean that every '(non)response' counts as relevantly not something in conversation?*

▷ *Consider what speaker A says in reaction to the '(non)response'. What kind of speech act is this? Does this utterance tell us anything about the relationship between the two speakers (i.e. strangers, acquaintances, or intimates)?*

Chapter 9
Discourse and culture

Text 20

JOHN GUMPERZ and JENNY COOK-GUMPERZ:
'Introduction: language and the communication of social
identity' in J. Gumperz (ed.): *Language and Social Identity*.
Cambridge University Press 1982, page 12

Although the pragmatic conditions of communicative tasks are
theoretically taken to be universal, the realizations of these tasks
as social practices are culturally variable. This variation can be
analyzed from several different perspectives, all of which of
course co-occur in the actual practices.

(1) Different cultural assumptions about the situation and
about appropriate behavior and intentions within it.

(2) Different ways of structuring information or an argument
in a conversation.

(3) Different ways of speaking: the use of a different set of
unconscious linguistic conventions (such as tone of voice)
to emphasize, to signal local connections and to indicate
the significance of what is being said in terms of overall
meaning and attitudes.

By 'different cultural assumptions' we refer to the fact that, even
though people in situations such as we study agree on the overall
purpose of the interaction, there are often radical differences as to
what expectations and rights are involved at any one time.

▷ *There is a suggestion here that 'pragmatic conditions' can be
treated as 'universal' (i.e. applicable everywhere). Can you
suggest some examples of pragmatic universals? How about
'Be polite'? Any others?*

▷ *Can you think of any examples that would support the idea
that 'appropriate behavior' differs in different cultures (pragmatically speaking)?*

▷ *Do you agree with these authors that there are different ways
of 'structuring an argument'? How is an argument structured
in English? How could it be structured any other way?*

Text 21

JENNY THOMAS: 'Cross-cultural pragmatic failure' in
Applied Linguistics 4/2, 1983, page 105

'Free goods' are those which, in a given situation, anyone can use
without seeking permission, for example, salt in a restaurant
(providing, of course, that you are having a meal in that restaurant and have not simply wandered in from the street with a bag of
fish and chips). Generally speaking, what an individual regards as
'free goods' varies according to relationships and situation. In
one's own family or home, most things (food, drink, books,
baths) are free goods. In a stranger's house they are not. Cross-
culturally, too, perceptions of what constitutes 'free' or 'nearly
free' goods differ. In Britain, matches are 'nearly free', so one
would not use a particularly elaborate politeness strategy to
request one, even of a total stranger. In the Soviet Union cigarettes
are also virtually 'free' and a request for them demands an equally
minimal degree of politeness, such as *Daite sigaretu [give (me) a
cigarette]*. A Russian requesting a cigarette in this country and
using a similar strategy would either have wrongly encoded the
amount of politeness s/he intended (covert grammatical or pragmalinguistic failure) or seriously misjudged the size of imposition
(sociopragmatic failure).

▷ *The author is writing ('in this country') about Britain. Do you
think her observation on salt in a restaurant is based on a universal component of a 'restaurant script'? In a family context,
do you agree that 'most things ... are treated as free goods'?
What about other cultures you are familiar with?*

▷ *The examples in this text are physical objects. There are also
cultural differences in what kind of information is considered
'free goods'. What constraints are there, in cultures you are
familiar with, on asking people about certain topics (for
example, their political views, religion, marital status,
income, cost of their possessions, bathroom behavior, sexual
practices)?*

▷ *What do think the distinction is between the two kinds of 'failure' (pragmalinguistic and sociopragmatic) described here?*

Text 22

DEBORAH TANNEN: *You Just Don't Understand.*
Wm. Morrow 1990, page 40

A woman was telling me why a long-term relationship had ended. She recounted a recurrent and pivotal conversation. She and the man she lived with had agreed that they would both be free, but they would not do anything to hurt each other. When the man began to sleep with other women, she protested, and he was incensed at her protest. Their conversation went like this:

SHE: How can you do this when you know it's hurting me?
HE: How can you try to limit my freedom?
SHE: But it makes me feel awful.
HE: You are trying to manipulate me.

On one level, this is simply an example of a clash of wills: What he wanted conflicted with what she wanted. But in a fundamental way, it reflects the difference in focus I have been describing. In arguing for his point of view, the key issue for this man was his independence, his freedom of action. The key issue for the woman was their interdependence—how what he did made her feel. He interpreted her insistence on their interdependence as 'manipulation': She was using her feelings to control his behavior.

▷ *Do you agree with the analysis presented here? Are there other implicatures possible from what is said in the dialog?*

▷ *We are used to thinking that the term 'cross-cultural' will apply to people from different countries. Is it appropriate to think of the interactions between males and females within one country (sharing a lot of one culture) as a site for the study of cross-cultural pragmatics? What kinds of differences might be worthy of investigation?*

SECTION 3
References

The references which follow can be classified into introductory level (marked ■□□), more advanced and consequently more technical (marked ■■□), and specialized, very demanding (marked ■■■).

Chapter 1
Definitions and background

■■■

STEVEN DAVIS (ed.): *Pragmatics. A Reader.*
Oxford University Press 1991

This is a collection of thirty-five papers, originally published in journals dealing mainly with philosophical issues in the recent history of pragmatics.

■□□

GEORGIA GREEN: *Pragmatics and Natural Language Understanding.* Lawrence Erlbaum 1989

This is an introduction which focuses on linguistic pragmatics as 'the study of understanding intentional human action', with a strong emphasis on grammatical issues.

■□□

GEOFFREY LEECH: *Principles of Pragmatics.*
Longman 1983

This introductory text presents a rhetorical model of pragmatics, attempting to describe 'principles and maxims of good communicative behaviour'. Pragmatics is defined as 'the study of how utterances have meanings in situations', with an emphasis on the analysis of politeness.

■■□

STEPHEN C. LEVINSON: *Pragmatics.*
Cambridge University Press 1983

This widely used introductory text offers several different definitions of pragmatics and presents 'an overview of some of the central tasks that pragmaticists wrestle with'. The emphasis is on linguistic and philosophical issues.

■□□

JACOB MEY: *Pragmatics: An Introduction.*
Blackwell 1993

This is a comprehensive introduction to pragmatics as 'the study of the conditions of human language use as these are determined by the context of society'. There is a strong emphasis on the ways in which society's institutions govern the use of language.

■□□

JAN NUYTS and JEF VERSCHUEREN (eds.):
A Comprehensive Bibliography of Pragmatics. Volumes 1–4.
John Benjamins 1987

This remarkable resource provides a wide range of references. The very useful diagrams in the Subject Index (pages 51–69) act as a guide to the wide areas of study covered by pragmatics.

Chapter 2
Deixis and distance

■■□

STEPHEN ANDERSON and EDWARD KEENAN: 'Deixis' in
Timothy Shopen (ed.): *Language Typology and Syntactic Description. Volume 3: Grammatical Categories and the Lexicon.* Cambridge University Press 1985

This paper presents a review of the range of deictic expressions used in a wide variety of languages.

■■□

ROBERT JARVELLA and WOLFGANG KLEIN (eds.): *Speech, Place and Action: Studies in Deixis and Related Topics.*
John Wiley & Sons 1982

This is a collection of fifteen papers on different aspects of deixis by both linguists and psychologists, incorporating studies on deixis and the blind and in the sign language of the deaf.

■■□

JOHN LYONS: *Natural Language and Universal Grammar.*
Cambridge University Press 1991

Chapters 8 and 9 in this collection of essays provide a lot of insights into the nature of deixis.

■□□

ROGER WALES: 'Deixis' in P. Fletcher and M. Garman (eds.): *Language Acquisition* (2nd edn.) Cambridge University Press 1986

This is a review paper covering studies of the first appearance and development of deictic forms in the early language of young children.

■■□

JURGEN WEISSENBORN and WOLFGANG KLEIN (eds.): *Here and There: Cross-linguistic Studies on Deixis and Demonstration.* John Benjamins 1982

This is a collection of fourteen papers on different types of deixis in a wide range of languages.

Chapter 3
Reference and inference

■■■

HERBERT CLARK and DEANNA WILKES-GIBBS: 'Referring as a collaborative process' in *Cognition* 22, 1986

This important paper presents evidence for the ways in which speakers in conversation collaborate to create referring expressions.

■■□

GILES FAUCONNIER: *Mental Spaces.*
Cambridge University Press 1994

This is a very original approach to the ways in which we connect words to referents, emphasizing the assumption of shared knowledge and the role of pragmatic connections.

■■□

TALMY GIVON: *Mind, Code and Context: Essays in Pragmatics.* Lawrence Erlbaum 1989

This collection of essays covers many topics in pragmatics, including reference (Chapters 5 and 6), from a perspective that emphasizes function (what language is used for).

■□□

JOHN LYONS: *Semantics.* Volume 1.
Cambridge University Press 1977

Chapter 7, on reference, sense, and denotation, presents a comprehensive background to the basic issues in the traditional semantic treatment of how words are used to refer.

■■■

GEOFFREY NUNBERG: *The Pragmatics of Reference.*
Indiana University Linguistics Club 1977

This dissertation uses the idea that words can be shown to have endless possible referents to argue for a pragmatic analysis in which word-meanings cannot be separated from 'knowledge of other kinds of conventions and social practices'.

Chapter 4
Presupposition and entailment

■■■

NOEL BURTON-ROBERTS: *The Limits to Debate. A Revised Theory of Semantic Presupposition.* Cambridge University Press 1989

This book represents one of the few recent attempts to reconsider the basic concepts involved in presupposition.

■■■

CHOON-KYU OH and DAVID DINEEN (eds.): *Syntax and Semantics Volume 11: Presupposition.* Academic Press 1979

This collection of sixteen papers, plus an extensive bibliography, illustrates the types of controversies surrounding the nature of presupposition. Many are presented in very technical language.

■■□

NEIL SMITH and DEIRDRE WILSON: *Modern Linguistics.* Penguin 1979

Chapters 7 and 8 of this text provide a detailed review of presupposition, entailment, and the role of ordered entailments.

■■■

ROB VAN DER SANDT: *Context and Presupposition.* Croom Helm 1988

This book reconsiders the connection between presupposition, context, and the projection problem.

Chapter 5
Cooperation and implicature

■□□

DIANE BLAKEMORE: *Understanding Utterances. An Introduction to Pragmatics.* Blackwell 1992

This is an introduction to pragmatics in which Relevance is taken to be the central concept.

■■■

LAURENCE HORN: 'Toward a new taxonomy for pragmatic inference: Q-based and R-based implicature' in Deborah Schiffrin (ed.): *Meaning, Form and Use in Context: Linguistic Applications.* Georgetown University Press 1984

This paper proposes an alternative approach to analyzing how implicatures arise, using two instead of four maxims.

■■□

PAUL GRICE: *Studies in the Way of Words.*
Harvard University Press 1989

This volume includes the collected papers of the philosopher whose ideas are considered by many to be the foundation of contemporary pragmatics.

■■■

Proceedings of the Berkeley Linguistic Society 16, 1990

There is a collection of sixteen papers, presented as a parasession within these published proceedings, on the legacy of Grice, covering a wide range of issues in the analysis of meaning.

■■□

DAN SPERBER and DEIRDRE WILSON: *Relevance.* Blackwell 1986

Presented as a study of human communication, this book takes the single maxim of Relevance as the key. Arguments and illustrations are presented to support the contention that 'communicated information comes with a guarantee of relevance'.

Chapter 6
Speech acts and events

■■□

J. AUSTIN: *How to Do Things with Words.* (2nd edn.)
Clarendon Press 1975

The original work which introduced the concept of language use as a form of action.

■□□

KENT BACH and ROBERT HARNISH: *Linguistic Communication and Speech Acts.* MIT Press 1979

Two linguists present a detailed framework for the analysis of speech acts.

■■□

JOHN SEARLE: *Speech Acts. An Essay in the Philosophy of Language*. Cambridge University Press 1969

The best known work on the topic, with detailed discussion of both conditions and applications of the concept of a speech act.

■■■

JOHN SEARLE: *Expression and Meaning. Studies in the Theory of Speech Acts*. Cambridge University Press 1979

A collection of seven papers, including one on indirect speech acts and another on a taxonomy of illocutionary acts. These frequently cited papers represent a development of the ideas presented earlier in Searle (1969).

■■□

JEF VERSCHUEREN: *What People Say They Do With Words*. Ablex 1985

This book presents a critical review of problems in speech act theory and a proposal for a different approach based on the study of linguistic action.

Chapter 7
Politeness and interaction

■■□

SHOSHANA BLUM-KULKA and GABRIELE KASPER: *Journal of Pragmatics* 14/2 (Special Issue on politeness), 1990

This collection of six papers includes a review paper by Kasper on current research issues as well as three reports on the development of politeness behavior in children.

■■□

PENELOPE BROWN and STEPHEN LEVINSON: *Politeness. Some Universals of Language Usage*. Cambridge University Press 1987

This is the most comprehensive book on linguistic politeness, offering lots of detailed discussion and illustrations from different languages.

■■□

PAUL DREW and JOHN HERITAGE (eds.): *Talk at Work: Interaction in Institutional Settings*. Cambridge University Press 1992

This is a collection of fifteen papers on the general topic of interaction in work contexts (for example, news interviews, court proceedings, doctor's office).

■□□

M. DUFON, G. KASPER, S. TAKAHASHI, and N. YOSHINAGA: 'Bibliography on Linguistic Politeness' in *Journal of Pragmatics* 21, 1994, pages 527–78

This is an extremely useful listing of published work concerned with language and politeness.

■■□

ERVING GOFFMAN: *Forms of Talk*. University of Pennsylvania Press 1981

This is a collection of five important papers by one of the most influential writers on language and social interaction.

Chapter 8
Conversation and preference structure

■■□

MAXWELL ATKINSON and JOHN HERITAGE (eds.): *Structures of Social Action: Studies in Conversation Analysis*. Cambridge University Press 1984

This is a collection of sixteen papers by some of the best known writers on conversation analysis.

■■□

JACK BILMES: 'The concept of preference in conversation analysis' in *Language in Society* 17, 1988

This paper presents a review of the uses of the term 'preference' and argues for a more precise application of the analytic concept.

■■□

ROBERT CRAIG and KAREN TRACY (eds.): *Conversational Coherence: Form, Structure and Strategy*. Sage 1983

This is a collection of fourteen papers on conversation as interpersonal communication, viewed from a range of perspectives.

■■□

HARVEY SACKS: *Lectures on Conversation*. Volumes 1–2. Blackwell 1992

These two volumes present the original lecture material in which the foundations of conversation analysis were established.

■■□

DEBORAH TANNEN: *Conversational Style: Analyzing Talk Among Friends*. Ablex 1984

This book presents extensive illustration of different aspects of conversational style as 'the basic tools with which people communicate'.

■■□

TEUN VAN DIJK: *Handbook of Discourse Analysis. Volume 3: Discourse and Dialogue*. Academic Press 1985

This volume contains sixteen papers illustrating a range of different perspectives on aspects of interactive talk.

Chapter 9
Discourse and culture

■■□

S.BLUM-KULKA, J.HOUSE, and G.KASPER (eds.): *Crosscultural Pragmatics: Requests and Apologies*. Ablex 1989

This is a collection of ten papers describing studies undertaken within the framework of the Cross-cultural Speech Act Realization Project.

■■□

GILLIAN BROWN and GEORGE YULE: *Discourse Analysis.*
Cambridge University Press 1983

This is a standard textbook with a linguistic focus on the study of discourse.

■■□

JOHN GUMPERZ: *Discourse Strategies.*
Cambridge University Press 1982

This is a collection of ten papers by one the most influential writers on social interaction and cross-cultural communication.

■■□

GABRIELE KASPER and SHOSHANA BLUM-KULKA (eds.):
Interlanguage Pragmatics. Oxford University Press 1993

This is a collection of eleven papers on various pragmatic aspects of second language learning.

■■□

DEBORAH SCHIFFRIN: *Approaches to Discourse.*
Blackwell 1994

This is a guide to several different frameworks for doing discourse analysis.

■■□

ANNA WIERZBICKA: *Cross-cultural Pragmatics. The Semantics of Human Interaction.* Mouton de Gruyter 1991

This is a book about how cultural values and norms shape different modes of interaction.

SECTION 4
Glossary

Page references to Section 1, Survey, are given at the end of each entry.

adjacency pair A sequence of two utterances by different speakers in conversation. The second is a response to the first, e.g. question–answer. [77]

anaphor The word, typically a pronoun, used to maintain **reference** to someone or something already mentioned, e.g. 'An old man was limping towards us. *He* slowly came into view.' [23]

antecedent The initial expression used to identify someone or something for which an **anaphor** is used later, e.g. '*An old man* was limping towards us. He slowly came into view.' [23]

attributable silence The absence of talk when a speaker is given the right to speak in conversation. [73]

attributive use Using an expression to identify someone or something without being committed to the existence of an actual person or thing, e.g. 'the first person to walk on Mars'. [18]

backchannels/backchannel signals Vocal indications of attention, e.g. 'uh-huh', 'hmm', when someone else is talking. [75]

background entailment Any logical consequence of an utterance. [33]

bald on record Utterances, e.g. orders, directly addressed to another where the **illocutionary force** is made explicit. [63]

cataphora The use of a word (typically a pronoun) to introduce someone or something that is more fully identified later, e.g. '*He* slowly came into view. An old man was limping towards us.' [23]

coherence The familiar and expected relationships in experience which we use to connect the meanings of utterances, even when those connections are not explicitly made. [84]

commissive A speech act in which the speaker commits him or herself to some future action, e.g. a promise. *See* Table 6.1. [54]

constancy under negation Quality of the **presupposition** of a statement remaining true when the statement is negated. [26]

content conditions In order to count as a particular type of speech act, an utterance must contain certain features, e.g. a promise must be about a future event. [50]

context The physical environment in which a word is used: cf. **co-text**. [21]

contrastive pragmatics The study of culturally different ways of using language. [88]

conventional implicature An additional unstated meaning associated with the use of a specific word, e.g. 'A but B' implies a contrast between A and B, so 'contrast' is a conventional implicature of 'but'. [45]

conversational implicature An additional unstated meaning that has to be assumed in order to maintain the **cooperative principle**, e.g. if someone says 'The President is a mouse', something that is literally false, the hearer must assume the speaker means to convey more than is being said. [40]

conversational style Particular way of participating in conversation. [76]

cooperative principle A basic assumption in conversation that each participant will attempt to contribute appropriately, at the required time, to the current exchange of talk. [37]

co-text The linguistic environment in which a word is used: cf. **context**. [21]

counterfactual presupposition The assumption that certain information is the opposite of true. [29]

cross-cultural pragmatics The study of different expectations among different communities regarding how meaning is constructed. [87]

cultural schemata Pre-existing knowledge structures based on experience in a particular culture. [87]

declaration A speech act that brings about a change by being uttered, e.g. a judge pronouncing a sentence. *See* Table 6.1. [53]

deference strategy Feature of interactive talk emphasizing **negative politeness**, the non-personal, and freedom from imposition. [66]

deictic center The speaker's location/time. [9]

deictic expression *See* **deixis**. [9]

deictic projection Speakers acting as if they are somewhere else. [13]

deixis 'Pointing' via language, using a **deictic expression**, e.g. 'this', 'here'. [9]

directive A speech act used to get someone else to do something, e.g. an order. *See* Table 6.1. [54]

direct speech act Speech act where a direct relationship exists between the structure and communicative function of an utterance, e.g. using an interrogative form ('Can you ... ?') to ask a question ('Can you swim?'): cf. **indirect speech act**. [55]

discourse analysis The study of language use with reference to the social and psychological factors that influence communication. [83]

dispreferred The structurally unexpected next utterance as a response, e.g. an invitation is normally followed by an acceptance, so a refusal is dispreferred. [79]

distal Away from the speaker, e.g. 'that', 'there': cf. **proximal**. [9]

ellipsis The absence of a word or words from a structural slot. [23]

entailment Something that logically follows from what is asserted. [25]

essential condition In performing a **speech act**, a requirement that the utterance commits the speaker to the act performed. [51]

exclusive 'we' Addressee excluded: cf. **inclusive 'we'**. [11]

existential presupposition An assumption that someone or something, identified by use of a noun phrase, does exist. [27]

explicit performative A **speech act** containing a **performative verb**: cf. **implicit performative**. [52]

expressive A speech act in which the speaker expresses feelings or attitudes, e.g. an apology. *See* Table 6.1. [53]

face A person's public self-image. [60]

face saving act Utterance or action which avoids a potential threat to a person's public self-image. [61]

face threatening act Utterance or action which threatens a person's public self-image. [61]

face wants A person's expectations that their public self-image will be respected. [61]

factive presupposition The assumption that information stated after certain words, e.g. 'know', 'regret', is true: cf. **non-factive presupposition**. [27]

felicity conditions The appropriate conditions for a **speech act** to be recognized as intended. [50]

first part The first utterance in an **adjacency pair**, e.g 'How are you?' *See also* **second part**. [77]

floor The current right to speak in a conversation. [72]

foreground entailment The main logical consequence of an utterance. [33]

frame A pre-existing knowledge structure with a fixed static pattern. [86]

general conditions Preconditions on performing a **speech act**. [50]

generalized conversational implicature An additional unstated meaning that does not depend on special or local knowledge: cf. **conversational implicature**. [41]

hedges Cautious notes expressed about how an utterance is to be taken, e.g. 'as far as I know' used when giving some information. [38]

high considerateness style A non-interrupting, non-imposing way of taking part in conversation. [76]

high involvement style An active, fast-paced, overlapping way of taking part in conversation. [76]

honorific Expression which marks that the addressee is of higher status. [10]

ideational function The use of language as a means of giving structure to thought and experience. [83]

Illocutionary Force Indicating Device (IFID) Indication in the speaker's utterance of the communicative force of that utterance. [49]

illocutionary act or **force** The communicative force of an utterance. [48]

implicature A short version of **conversational implicature**. [35]

implicit performative A **speech act** without a **performative verb**: cf. **explicit performative**. [52]

inclusive 'we' Speaker and addressee included: cf. **exclusive 'we'**. [11]

indexicals Like **deictic** expressions, forms used for 'pointing' via language. *See* **deixis**. [9]

indirect speech act Speech act where an indirect relationship exists between the structure and communicative function of an utterance, e.g. the use of an interrogative ('Can you … ?') not to ask a question, but to make a request ('Can you help me with this?'): cf. **direct speech act**. [55]

inference The listener's use of additional knowledge to make sense of what is not explicit in an utterance. [17]

insertion sequence A two part sequence that comes between the first and second parts of another sequence in conversation. [77]

interlanguage pragmatics The study of how non-native speakers communicate in a second language. [88]

interpersonal function The use of language for maintaining social roles and taking part in social interaction. [83]

lexical presupposition The assumption that, in using one word, the speaker can act as if another meaning (word) will be understood. [28]

local management system A metaphor for describing the conventions for organizing the right to speak in conversation. [72]

locutionary act The basic act of uttering a meaningful linguistic form. [48]

manner One of the **maxims**, in which the speaker is to be clear, brief, and orderly. *See* Table 5.1. [39]

maxim One of the four sub-principles of the **cooperative principle**. *See* **manner, quantity, quality**, and **relation**. *See also* Table 5.1. [37]

mitigating device Expression used to soften an imposition, e.g. 'please'. [63]

negative face The need to be independent, not imposed on by others: cf. **positive face**. [61]

negative politeness Awareness of another's right not to be imposed on: cf. **positive politeness**. [62]

negative politeness strategy An attempt to demonstrate awareness of another's right not to be imposed on: cf. **positive politeness strategy**. [64]

non-factive presupposition The assumption that certain information, as presented, is not true: cf. **factive presupposition**. [29]

off record Utterances not directly addressed to another. [63]

on record Utterances directly addressed to another. [63]

overlap More than one speaker talking at the same time in conversation. [72]

particularized conversational implicature An additional unstated meaning that depends on special or local knowledge: cf. **conversational implicature**. [42]

performative hypothesis A proposal that, underlying every utterance, there is a clause with a verb that identifies the **speech act**. [51]

performative verb A verb that explicitly names the **speech act**, e.g. the verb 'promise' in the utterance 'I promise to be there'. [49]

perlocutionary act/effect The effect of an utterance used to perform a **speech act**. [48, 49]

person deixis Forms used to point to people, e.g. 'me', 'you'. [9]

politeness Showing awareness of another person's public self-image **face wants**. [60]

positive face The need to be connected, to belong to a group: cf. **negative face**. [62]

positive politeness Showing solidarity with another: cf. **negative politeness**. [62]

positive politeness strategy An appeal to solidarity with another: cf. **negative politeness strategy**. [64]

potential presupposition An assumption typically associated with use of a linguistic form, e.g. the use of the verb 'regret' in 'He regrets doing that' carries an assumption that he actually 'did that'. [27]

pragmatic accent Aspects of talk that indicate what is assumed to be communicated without being said. [88]

pragmatic connection A conventional association between a person's name and a kind of object, e.g. 'Shakespeare' used to identify a book. [20]

pragmatics The study of speaker meaning as distinct from word or sentence meaning. [4]

pre-announcement Utterance before an announcement to check if an announcement can be made. [68]

preference/preference structure A pattern in which one type of utterance will be more typically found in response to another in a conversational sequence, e.g. an acceptance will more typically follow an invitation than a refusal. [79]

preferred The structurally expected next utterance used in a response. [79]

pre-invitation Utterance before an invitation to check if an invitation can be made. [68]

preparatory conditions Specific requirements prior to an utterance in order for it to count as a particular **speech act**. [50]

pre-request Utterance before a request to check if a request can be made. [67]

presupposition Something the speaker assumes to be the case. [25]

primary performative An utterance which performs a **speech act** but which does not contain a **performative verb**. [52]

projection problem The problem of the **presupposition** of a simple structure not surviving when part of a more complex structure. [30]

proximal Near speaker, e.g. 'this', 'here': cf. **distal**. [9]

psychological distance Speaker's marking of how close or distant something is perceived to be. [13]

quality One of the **maxims**, in which the speaker has to be truthful. *See* Table 5.1. [38]

quantity One of the **maxims**, in which the speaker has to be neither more or less informative than is necessary. *See* Table 5.1. [38]

range of reference All the possible referents identifiable by use of a word. [21]

reference An act by which a speaker uses a word, or words, to enable a listener to identify someone or something. [17]

referential use Using an expression to identify someone or something when the person or thing is assumed to be known: cf. **attributive use**. [18]

referring expression A linguistic form which enables a listener, or reader, to identify something. [17]

relation One of the **maxims**, in which the speaker has to be relevant. *See* Table 5.1.

representative A **speech act** in which the speaker states what is believed or known, e.g. an assertion. *See* Table 6.1. [53]

scalar implicature An additional meaning of the negative of any value higher on a scale than the one uttered, e.g. in saying 'some children', I create an implicature that what I say does not apply to 'all children'. [41]

schema (plural **schemata**) A pre-existing knowledge structure in memory typically involving the normal expected patterns of things, e.g. an apartment schema has a kitchen, a bedroom, etc. [85]

script A pre-existing knowledge structure for interpreting event sequences, e.g. a visit to the dentist has a script of specific events in sequence (which might start with giving one's name to the receptionist and finish with making a further appointment). [86]

second part The second or response utterance in an adjacency pair, e.g. 'Fine, thanks'. *See* **first part**. [77]

semantics The study of how words literally connect to things, or more generally, the investigation of meaning as encoded in language. [4]

sincerity conditions Requirements on the genuine intentions of a speaker in order for an utterance to count as a particular **speech act**. [51]

social deixis Forms used to indicate relative social status. [10]

solidarity strategy An emphasis on the closeness of speaker and addressee. [65]

spatial deixis Forms used to point to location, e.g. 'here', 'there': cf. **temporal deixis**. [9]

speech act An action performed by the use of an utterance to communicate. [47]

speech event A set of circumstances in which people interact in some conventional way to arrive at some outcome. [47, 57]

structural presupposition The assumption that part of a structure contains information being treated as already known. [28]

syntax The study of the structures connecting linguistic forms. [4]

tautology An apparently meaningless expression in which one word is defined as itself, e.g. 'business is business'. [35]

temporal deixis Forms used to point to location in time, e.g. 'now', 'then': cf. **spatial deixis.** [9]

textual function The use of language in the creation of well-formed text. [83]

Transition Relevance Place (TRP) A possible change of speaker point in an interaction. [72]

turn The opportunity to speak at some point during a conversation. [72]

turn-taking The change of speaker during conversation. [72]

T/V distinction A distinction between forms used for a familiar (*'tu'*) and a non-familiar (*'vous'*) addressee, in French and other languages. [10]

zero anaphora The absence of an expression in a structural slot where one is assumed, as a way of maintaining reference, e.g. 'Mary mowed the lawn and then _ watered it.' [23]

Acknowledgements

The author and publisher are grateful to the following for permission to reproduce extracts from copyright material:

Academic Press, Inc. and the authors for extracts from Gerald Gazdar: *Pragmatics. Implicature, Presupposition, and Logical Form* (1979); J. L. Morgan: 'Two types of convention in indirect speech acts' in Peter Cole (ed.): *Syntax and Semantics Volume 9: Pragmatics* (1978).

Basic Books, a division of HarperCollins Publishers, Inc. for an extract from Robin Tolmach Lakoff: *Talking Power: The Politics of Language,* copyright ® 1990 by Robin Tolmach Lakoff.

Blackwell Publishers for an extract from Harvey Sacks: *Lectures on Conversation* (1992).

Cambridge University Press and the authors for extracts from Penelope Brown and Stephen Levinson: *Politeness* (1987); John Gumperz and Jenny Cook-Gumperz: 'Introduction: language and the communication of social identity' in J. Gumperz (ed.): *Language and Social Identity* (1982); John Searle: *Speech Acts* (1969).

Elsevier Science Ltd., The Boulevard, Langford Lane, Kidlington OX5 1GB, UK for an extract from Gabriele Kasper: 'Politeness' in Ron Asher (ed.): *The Encyclopedia of Language and Linguistics* Volume 6 (1994), copyright ® 1994.

Lawrence Erlbaum Associates, Inc. and the author for an extract from Georgia Green: *Pragmatics and Natural Language Understanding* (1989).

Charles Fillmore for an extract from Charles Fillmore: *Santa Cruz Lectures on Deixis* (Indiana University Linguistics Club 1975).

Kathleen Grice for an extract from Paul Grice: 'Logic and conversation' in P. Cole and J. Morgan (eds.): *Syntax and Semantics Volume 3: Speech Acts* (1975).

Kluwer Academic Publishers for extracts from Geoffrey Nunberg: 'Indexicality and deixis' in *Linguistics and Philosophy* 16 (1993); Quentin Smith 'The multiple uses of indexicals' in *Synthese* 78 (1989).

The Linguistics Society of America for extracts from Harvey Sacks *et al.*: 'A simplest systematics for the organization of turn-taking in conversation' in *Language* 50 (1974).

Longman Group Ltd. for extracts from M.A.K. Halliday and Ruqaiya Hasan: *Cohesion in English* (1976); Geoffrey Leech: *Principles of Pragmatics* (1983).

Wm. Morrow for an extract from Deborah Tannen: *You Just Don't Understand* (1990).

New York University Press for an extract from Robert C. Stalnaker: 'Pragmatic presupposition' in Milton Munitz and Peter Unger (eds.): *Semantics and Philosophy* (1974).

The Ohio State University Press for an extract from: 'Pragmatics: meaning and context' File 70 in *Language Files: Materials for an Introduction to Linguistics* (6th edn.), the Ohio State University Department of Linguistics, edited by Stefanie Jannedy, Robert Poletto, and Tracey L. Weldon, copyright ® 1994 by the Ohio State University Press. All rights reserved.

Oxford University Press for an extract from Jenny Thomas: 'Cross cultural pragmatic failure' in *Applied Linguistics* 4/2 (1983).

Plenum Publishing Corporation and the author for an extract from Jack Bilmes: *Discourse and Behaviour* (1986).

Despite every effort to trace and contact copyright holders before publication, this has not always been possible. If notified, the publisher will be pleased to rectify any errors or omissions at the earliest opportunity.